The Fishing Life

The Fishing Life

An Angler's Tales of Wild Rivers and
Other Restless Metaphors

PAUL SCHULLERY

Illustrations by
Marsha Karle

SKYHORSE PUBLISHING

Skyhorse Publishing books may be purchased in bulk at special discounts for sales promotion, corporate gifts, fund-raising, or educational purposes. Special editions can also be created to specifications. For details, contact the Special Sales Department, Skyhorse Publishing, 307 West 36th Street, 11th Floor, New York, NY 10018 or info@skyhorsepublishing.com.

Skyhorse® and Skyhorse Publishing® are registered trademarks of Skyhorse Publishing, Inc.®, a Delaware corporation.

Visit our website at www.skyhorsepublishing.com.

10 9 8 7 6 5 4 3 2 1

Library of Congress Cataloging-in-Publication Data is available on file.

ISBN: 978-1-61608-838-5

Printed in the United States of America

For Andrew Herd, angler, historian, and friend

TABLE OF CONTENTS

Fishing for trout, I have often thought, is a little more like life than actual living is.

Odell Shepard

Our tradition is that of the first man who sneaked away to the creek when the tribe did not really need fish.

Roderick Haig-Brown

PREFACE

I'M SURE there are plenty of writers whose output slips into such tidy
pigeonholes that a book like this is never possible, much less necessary.
Mine doesn't. For the past thirty years or so, in a perhaps naïve attempt
to share the joys of the fisherman's world with everyone else, I have
scattered stories about fish and fishing in books and articles that were
aimed at, well, everyone else.

I have always considered the integration of fish and fishing into my
books about natural history, conservation, and other subjects a good
and important thing. For one thing, writing across traditional literary
boundaries prevents what Arnold Gingrich, the popular angling commentator of the 1960s and 1970s, once called "hardening of the categories." But it has also also left me with the disappointed feeling that
some of my very favorite fishing stories were missing the people I'd
most want to read them.

I'm delighted, then, that thanks to the courtesy of some publishers and a fortuitous realignment of the copyright stars, this errant
material, supplemented and I hope complemented with some items
I'd been saving up for such an opportunity, has become available for
a book of its own. I am just as pleased to discover that these stories,
essays, farces, daydreams, screeds, and ruminations so happily formed

themselves into just the sort of quirky reflection on the fishing life that I hoped they would. Fishing has many moods—not just good or bad, but whimsical, reflective, silly, inquisitive, lazy, demanding, and once in a while downright strange. As I hope this book suggests, I wouldn't have it any other way.

The Fishing Life

Introduction

ON MONSTERS

ONCE IN the mid-1950s, when we lived on the south Texas coast, my family went for a picnic along the Nueces River. My mother and sister didn't care much for fishing, but my dad and my older brother did, and I was just interested enough that they usually took me with them, if only to prevent me whining about not getting to go. Steve was about twelve, and I was seven or so.

I don't think we caught anything from the Nueces, but of all the places that we fished when I was small, the Nueces was the one that most formed my idea of what fishing could be—not a way to gather food, or have fun, or get exercise, but a sort of quest. The Nueces, unlike everyplace else we fished where really big fish were just an idle dream or something we somehow knew only others would catch, had fish so huge that I was frightened to get close to the water.

We saw evidence of them along the shore. Fireplaces and picnic spots were littered with big, shiny, flat things—in my memory, they were the size of Chevy hubcaps—that I was stunned to discover were scales. I knew only the dainty little scales of bluegills, and I remember not fully believing that there could be a fish big enough to need more than one or two of these dinner plates per side. I had no idea.

We fished at a deep, wide, still stretch of river. I don't remember fishing at all, though I suppose I did. I do remember watching my dad—a big, broad, and very strong man—stand along the bank lobbing a hefty chunk of weighted shrimp or some other meat out into the current with his old casting rod. I remember the shore was dusty, and, like everyplace else in Texas, it was hot.

Mostly, though, I remember the gar. Alligator gar have grown to more than 300 pounds, more than nine feet long. I don't suppose the ones we saw were that big, but even allowing for the amplification of memory, they must have been four or five feet. Let's say five. Maybe six. Maybe I'd better admit it: I still think they were at least ten. Out in the middle of the river, about as far as my dad could cast, one would roll every now and then, an immense churning turn on the surface, baring its dully glinting back for a moment to the bright Texas sun.

Even at that age, I had seen big fish. From the wharves near Corpus Christi, my dad had pointed out the moving fins of tarpon and sharks, and I'd seen big hammerheads taken from the pier at Padre Island. But that was the ocean, where, given enough horizon, nothing looks too big. In the Nueces—at that place, at that age, and at that distance—the gar was more monster than fish. My clearest memory of all is of the moment following the fish's roll, when my dad would put his considerable muscle into a cast aimed right at the still-swirling spot where the fish had just surfaced. I was scared beyond words that he would hook the fish and it would pull him in.

Here was fishing with proof for the effort. When those big fish rose and pushed against the boundary between their world and mine, they very nearly fulfilled the fisherman's dream merely by satisfying the hope we all have that there really is a chance, however faint, of catching a monster—because the monsters were really there.

Memory of the gar came back to me many years later along a small stream in the Yellowstone backcountry. I was introducing two friends to some of the techniques of fly fishing, making a few casts to show them where to find fish and what to do about it. I stood at a long, still pool, where the water was a little murky and the far bank was thirty or forty feet away. Counseling my companions to watch closely, I cast a streamer across the stream at a downstream angle, so that the large fly splashed into the shallows along the far shore. I then began a series of quick, jerky retrieves, pulling the line through the guides and the fly back toward me across the deep pool.

When the fly was about a third of the way back to me, a good-sized trout swirled to the surface behind it, lunged at it, and turned back into the deep water. With some excitement in my voice (nothing makes a fishing lesson more instructive than a fish), I said, "See that?"

Both my friends stared blankly at the water. "What?"

They had been looking at the water. They had been following the progress of the fly with considerable interest. But neither had known what they were looking for. The swirl of the fish, into which I had read so much meaning, had not even registered.

I, on the other hand, having spent a few thousand hours looking at the surfaces of lakes and streams since that day on the Nueces, had grown to assume that this stuff was visible to everyone. Jolted back into reality, and a little surprised at how completely I'd lost touch with the nonspecialist's perspective, I made a poor attempt at explaining how a fish will disturb the surface when it moves, whether it moves for food or flight or other reasons. But what I most wish I could have conveyed to them was the thrill the observant fisherman finds in these surface disturbances. In their urgent immediacy, they give promise of the strike we yearn for, yet in their indistinct disruption of the surface they reach deeper into our hopes, where monsters lurk and dreams await realization.

This is a book about such intense moments, and it is also a book about all those long stretches of thinking, hoping, daydreaming, and otherwise getting ready that occupy fishermen between those moments. Fishing—in my case fly fishing—is an opportunity to exercise our intellects and emotions in a realm of inexhaustible wonder. At any given moment we may think we're in this for just one thing, say the challenge of a difficult fish or the companion-ships of a fishing trip. But I suspect that most of the time we're in it for everything we can get, and we're out there just to see what will develop.

Angling's sages have often recommended patience as sport's foremost prerequisite, but that advice has been reduced to parody in the image of some serenely oblivious duffer, cane pole propped in a forked stick, asleep on the river bank, waiting, waiting, waiting. That's not a bad way to spend the day. It has charms of its own, and I've known people who raised it to the level of performance art.

But for many of us, the angler's patience is of a different sort. The angler waits, but with an energy, attentiveness, and athleticism that are, when practiced well, and in tune with your temperament, almost reward enough for the day.

But just almost. Greater rewards await. Once you're tuned in, once you're paying that kind of attention, something will develop. It may not be what you planned or hoped for, and it may happen when you are at your most relaxed and seemingly inattentive, but that's the great serendipitous joy of any pursuit carried on in the natural world. If you're a fisherman, the longer you look, the greater the hold that living, moving water will have on your imagination. There will be in the water's rolling motion half-heard promises, rumors of dark shapes, a vague feeling of answers withheld. But if you keep at it long enough, one day you may witness some greater disturbance, some rushing breach of the water's surface so startling and violent and exhilarating that you too will suddenly, and always thereafter, believe in monsters.

Part One:
Home and Away

Chapter One

MY GREAT FISHING ADVENTURE

ABOUT FORTY years ago, a friend and I, being in our early twenties and therefore without sense, decided to drive to Panama (and back, of course; we did realize we'd have to drive back). We lived in Ohio at the time, and had previously made several lengthy driving trips around the United States, once even venturing into near-Canada, but we longed for bigger game. We settled on Panama when persistent inquiry established that it was impossible to drive to Europe.

The somewhat hazy scope of this enterprise is revealed in our Secret Plan, which we didn't share even with our families. Our Secret Plan was not only to drive to Panama, but on our return trip to continue up the west coast of the United States and on into British Columbia as far as Prince Rupert or some similarly remote location, from which we would catch a plane to Alaska—whatever point of that state happened to be closest.

We were a little vague on the precise location of Alaska, but this didn't matter because we didn't actually want to see it. We only wanted to be able to say we'd been there. I imagined that our flight north from Prince Rupert would be in some ancient, rusty, and enormously picturesque aerial tugboat in which our only companions would be

a few ripe and scruffy old sourdoughs, some equally savory mala-
mutes, and perhaps a vacationing walrus or two.

But first there was all of Mexico and Central America to explore.
I had my fishing tackle with me as we set out from Ohio and was
dreaming of exotic sub-tropical fish. These fantasy creatures were
all shaped more or less like largemouth bass because that was the
only fish I had yet caught in my life that I knew had any caché
among real angling experts. But my Central American dream
bass had eerily shifting kaleidoscopic colors and flamboyantly
large fins and other mysterious, razor-edged appurtenances hanging randomly from their sides, and weighed fifteen to twenty-five
pounds. Three of them could strip a domestic cow to the bone in
four minutes. I was pretty sure about the cow, based on many years
of research watching highly authentic jungle adventure movies in
which such fish routinely dismantled expendable cast members,
sometimes taking on entire safari lines of movie extras at once.
I never actually saw the fish in these movies, but their behavior
pretty clearly defined their appearance for me. I did wonder if
such violent feeding might be hard on my tackle, but otherwise
remained optimistic.

Ohio in those days didn't prepare one for faraway fishing adventures. It didn't prepare one for catching fish, period. Ohio was, after
all, home of the Cuyahoga River, darkest legend among lovers of
American rivers for having been so thick with the filth of indus-
trial Cleveland that it was famously said to have caught fire and
burned vigorously for some time. I never fished the Cuyahoga, but
the slack-water Ohio impoundments I did fish could not have been
much better treated by the barbaric cretins who ruled the regional
industries. Even if there were fish surviving in these waters, the
wretched things wouldn't have been able to see my lures and baits
through the swirling asteroid fields of human excrement. These
were dark times.

My little tackle box contained my beloved Garcia Mitchell 300,
an extra spool of ancient line I didn't trust enough ever to use
but always kept handy, a spectacularly unreliable pocket knife, a

snake-bite kit, and a few rubber worms (purple with a white stripe). Most important, there were about a dozen treasured lures, the flagship of the fleet being a Johnson Silver Minnow, a kind of chrome Porsche among lures. There was no water in Ohio into which I would willingly have cast this lure. It cost too much and was far too beautiful. But who knew what magical place I might find on such a trip—a misty tropical river, a travel-poster coral reef, even a bear-lined Alaskan salmon stream—where this precious lure might justly be used? Not me.

Our Secret Plan, I might explain, was set aside on the return trip, late one evening in the Sonoran Desert not far south (sixty-nine kilometers, to be rigorously precise) of Nogales on the Mexico-Arizona border. We started out that morning from Mazatlan, and after covering about six hundred miles, we had just decided that we might as well drive all night and get to Ensenada by dawn (twelve thousand miles into the trip, we hadn't gotten noticeably brighter), when I accidentally put the little white Beetle into a high-speed spin while reaching behind me for the crackers. The road being empty for miles, and we being the only people foolish enough to drive at night there, we skidded along handsomely and without unpleasant interruption. We had come almost to a complete stop when the car slid off the shoulder of the pavement, and the sixty-nine-kilometer post caught the running board amidships. The milepost broke, but just enough of our momentum remained to roll us over upside down. It took a few days of negotiating with the *federales* and other local officials in Hermosillo over the necessary insurance paperwork—and to overcome the unspoken but apparently forceful conviction on their part that we were under arrest—but then we drove the car another three hundred miles back into the United States, to Tucson, Arizona, where it was declared "totalled" and traded in on a brand new Beetle. I was now somewhere well beyond broke, so we sadly abandoned Prince Rupert and the gamey aerial sourdoughs and hurried home to Ohio.

I did salvage at least one of my fantasy fishing episodes, however. Back before we'd left Ohio, our parents, trying to help us through what they surely must have seen as a nightmarish episode in idiotic young manhood (they had raised us, after all, and felt the pain of our magnificent blitheness), encouraged us to stop and see one our community's prominent citizens, who by wondrous coincidence also had a place in Central America, right along our route. Mr. Gesling, as we all called him, was a highly prosperous building contractor there in Ohio—so prosperous that he also owned one of the largest cattle ranches in the charming and peaceful country of Costa Rica. Learning of our planned trip, he heartily invited us to come and stay a few days with him.

We found his place easily, rather the way someone sailing west from, say, Europe, might find North America. It was some miles off the InterAmerican Highway, stretching beyond sight across the plains. But it wasn't, we soon realized, just a huge cattle ranch. It was rather like a duchy, or a fiefdom. Mr. Gesling, a large, florid man who could only have been played, in any meaningful movie of his life, by Wallace Beery, presided over the land with a gentle but clearly absolute authority. One morning, as we watched Mr. Gesling's son and some of his *peones* (his name for the cowboys) heading off with their horses and rifles in search of some pesky cattle rustlers, I began to realize how genuinely independent a really large amount of money could make someone in a charming and peaceful little country like this.

This realization was reinforced when I asked Mr. Gesling about the fishing. We had to this point gone about eight thousand miles. I had, through my vast ignorance and studied inattentiveness, already passed up perhaps a hundred extraordinary opportunities for memorable fishing. I know this now, but I have no recollection of even mentally registering the fishing possibilities of a variety of Mexican lakes and rivers, various coastal beaches from Vera Cruz to Belize (Belize, for Heaven's sake!), all the waterways associated with the Panama Canal, and a relentless succession of smaller waters—jungle, plain, and mountain—that would probably now cost your wealthy angling tourist a lien on his firstborn to fish.

But standing there on the shady, breezy, paradisiacal veranda of Mr. Gesling's rancho, looking down through the banana trees behind the kitchen building, I noticed a genuinely lovely little river and finally remembered my Mitchell 300. I told Mr. Gesling I thought I'd like to fish that river and asked if it would be okay with him. He said yes. Being even then a hard-core Goody Two-shoes, I admitted that I did not have a fishing license and wondered aloud what I should do. He smiled his benevolent Wallace-Beery smile and said, entirely without pretense or bombast, "Well, I'm kind of the law around here." I went fishing.

There was a ford across the river just behind the house, where his *peones* routinely churned up the current as they crossed on their horses. I hauled my tackle box down there and self-consciously rigged up my little pack rod and reel. Why I should be self-conscious thousands of miles from home with no one in sight, I don't know. It came on right away and stayed with me until I quit. Perhaps I sensed I was out of my element, as well as my league.

It was, I now realize, the worst, least-promising place on the river to fish, what with all the horsey disturbance, the blazing midday sun, the shallow water, and the bright-sand bottom. Even back then, I did know a little about what made a good fishing spot, and clearly this wasn't it. But both shorelines stretched off from this comfortingly open spot in lush, frondy, impenetrable, and profoundly snakey-looking riparian diversity, so I stayed right near the ford.

Now that the time had come and I was about to fish in a semitropical dream river, my sense of proportion took firm hold and I knew what I must do. I put on the Johnson Silver Minnow. It all seemed so momentous that I was prepared to lose this personal treasure in the mouth of the first bass-like monster I hooked, whatever its colors or bizarre accessories. I realized, not without a twinge of regret, that such a loss would probably be worth it, just to see the big brilliantly colored bassish thing swirl to the surface and shatter all this charming and peaceful country scenery for a moment.

Of course I needn't have worried about my precious Johnson Sil-ver Minnow. I still have it today—Costa Rica was not impressed. Nothing hit it. Nothing happened at all, not even an ominous swirl behind it as I retrieved it (as I have already suggested, I can milk the memory of an ominous swirl for years of fruitful daydreams). I made a bunch of casts, watched some *peones* ride by through the ominous fronds on the other shore, made some more casts, looked behind me for stalking jaguars, made some more casts, and called it a fishing trip.

(Aside: In order to ensure the accuracy of the previous paragraph, I went looking for that old tackle box, which I found after only forty-five minutes of rummaging through every closet on four floors. I do, indeed, still have the Johnson Silver Minnow, though it and a twin of it that I don't recall owning—perhaps they reproduce, like amoebae?—have now become a mottled, tarnished gum-wrapper-yellow. But here's an important safety tip: Never, under any circum-stances, allow your tackle box to sit unopened in warm places for fifteen years.)

I reeled in my Johnson Silver Minnow, wondering when lunch would be ready. Looking back, I suspect that I accepted my angling defeat with unseemly haste, but at the time there were other forces at work, such as fear of loathsome frond-dwelling creatures, that helped drive me from the water. Only days earlier, my pal and I had been, for no reason we ever understood, at gunpoint in a consid-erably less charming and peaceful little country just to the north. Macho teenaged boys dressed in U.S. Army surplus uniforms and waving automatic weapons around were somehow more, well, *imag-inable* than whatever might be lurking there in the fronds.

Besides, I could tell almost immediately that I wasn't going to catch anything. It felt strangely like Ohio in that respect, where "going fishing" had taken on an almost Zen level of disassociation from the word "fish." Sensing that no amount of additional effort was going to pay off, I probably reasoned that by quitting quickly I could at least claim not to have tried very hard. This is the subtle but effective gambit of "Oh, I wasn't really in the mood to stick with it," with its implication that I could have caught fish if I'd really wanted to bother, and its further implication that this river was somehow a little beneath my standards. My failure could only become more pronounced and embarrassing if I kept fishing. I reeled in and left.

Later, back in the rancho, when Mr. Gesling asked me how the fishing was, I just said I didn't catch anything. Rather than make the correct assumption that I was fishing like a dolt, this generous man thought about it for a moment and explained that there could hardly have been many fish in the river anyway. A volcano had erupted somewhere upstream just the year before, he explained, and killed all of them.

Naturally, I was eager to hear this. Though I have always been puzzled that it didn't occur to him to mention this stupendous disaster when I first asked about the fishing, it was and still is the most glamorous excuse for getting skunked I ever heard. I embraced it immediately, and have treasured it ever since.

Even so, I've often daydreamed about Mr. Gesling's little river since then. Well, it started as a daydream. Now I see it as a thirty-year sentimental inquiry into the quirks and vicissitudes of the angling life, all symbolized for me in that one day in Costa Rica. It was, in fact, pivotal in my fishing life. It signaled the close of my Ohio misadventures in lousy, violently abused fisheries. It became the opening scene in a much more dramatic fishing life than I'd known or even dreamed of. Shortly after my return, I began work as a park ranger in the mountains of Wyoming. I immediately began fly fishing, which I eventually did all over the country. Doing so, I discovered that there are many fishing waters so full of beautiful, energetic fish that I could expect to catch them with some regularity. Ohio receded, lost its power, and became a slightly melancholy but increasingly entertaining little memory.

But in those daydreams of Costa Rica, I still wonder what might have happened if I'd kept fishing that pretty little river—if I'd braved the frondy banks and poked around until I found a shady pool, or a riffled bend, and pitched the Johnson Silver Minnow into such a spot. Forty years on, I suppose that despite Mr. Gesling's kind provision of such a perfect excuse for my failure to catch anything, I prefer to believe there *were* fish in his river after all, and that if I'd stuck with it, one of them might have finally seen my Johnson Silver Minnow and come for it. A river without fish, though a great excuse for failure to catch anything, is considerably less appealing to an angling nostalgist than is a river whose fish were simply missed.

I guess that's how it goes with great adventures. When they're happening, they don't really last that long or necessarily even amount to much, but with a little luck and the right kind of imagination, we can go on enjoying them forever. And though at the time it may have seemed to me that this was in its odd, quiet way, quite an adventure, in fact my great fishing adventure had just begun.

Chapter Two

HOME RIVER

FISHING HAS a reputation as an innocuous, fairly mindless pastime enjoyed most by shiftless people. Perhaps that impression would be lessened if nonfishers understood more about wild water. Calling fishing a hobby is like calling brain surgery a job.

The average visitor driving through Yellowstone National Park sees no farther than the surface of the water. At best, the lakes and streams are mirrors reflecting the surrounding scenery. For the alert fisherman, especially the fly-fisherman, the surface is not a mirror but a window. Drive through Hayden Valley, along the Yellowstone River. If you aren't a fisher, you'll see many things, but the river, except where it is ridden by waterfowl or waded by moose, will rarely enter your thoughts, much less stimulate your spirit.

It's different if you fish. The surface of the water tells a story: that hump followed by a series of lessening ripples (if they were larger, they would be called standing waves) is proof of a rock or a stump submerged below. Those boulders on the far shore break the current, which moves slower close to them as the rock catches and retards it; fish and smaller creatures press themselves close to such obstructions to ease the labor of maintaining position in the current. The quiet eddies behind this log jam are home for schools of minnows and the occasional dragonfly nymph that will feed on them if it gets a chance. Soft swirls and rings on the river's surface are made by trout rising gently to inhale newly hatched mayflies and other insects floating on the surface as their wings dry. This water is a wilderness of its own, full of life we do not know and beauties we have not imagined. The fisherman is not unique in appreciating it—any good naturalist finds it enchanting—but the fisherman has found special ways of becoming involved in it.

In 1972, just a couple months after returning from Costa Rica, I was hired to work as a ranger-naturalist in Yellowstone. I was stationed at park headquarters at Mammoth Hot Springs in the northern part of the park. From there I began to explore this magnificent, magical place, and one of the first things I discovered was a river I instantly, even reflexively, adopted as my own. Or perhaps it adopted me. Either way, it became my home river.

The Gardner River is a small rocky stream born at about 9,000 feet in the Gallatin Mountains a few miles southwest of Mammoth. In its entire length of about twenty miles, it drops more than 3,500 feet to its mouth at Gardiner, Montana, where it joins the Yellowstone River (because of a quirk of history, the town is spelled with an "i" and the river is not). It flows from its headwaters pond at first north, then east, then southeast to its junction with Indian Creek at Indian Creek Campground, where it crosses under its first bridge, the road from Mammoth Hot Springs to Norris Geyser Basin. After this brief encounter with civilization, it runs east and then north, around what we call the "back" of Bunsen Peak, where it drops into its little-traveled canyon. Far below the vertical basaltic cliffs, the river gurgles along, pouring 150 feet in one jump over Osprey Falls and out across the eastern foot of Bunsen Peak. It passes under another bridge, the Mammoth-to-Tower road, and almost immediately is joined from the southeast by Lava Creek, which has just left its own canyon. The greater flow then follows the west foot of Mt. Everts almost due north until it dumps, rather privately, into the Yellowstone River right at the park boundary in Gardiner.

I caught my first trout from the Gardner. When my brother, a fly-fisherman of long commitment and great learning, heard that I was going to work in Yellowstone, he forced into my hands a complete fishing outfit, insisting that I learn to fly-fish and initiating me in a pastime that has at times been more a way of life than a sport. That first time, however, I was so intimidated by all the new devices and techniques that I was busy fiddling with the reel when a hungry little brown trout grabbed the fly I was paying no attention to, and I landed him only after considerable discussion and with relief that I'd chosen such a private spot for my first outing.

It turned out, as I was then just discovering, that fly-fishing is genuinely unlike other types of fishing. The flies—usually small, delicate imitations of various forms of insect life, made of feathers, hair, and yarn tied to a small hook—have practically no weight. They cannot be cast with a spinning or casting rod like other lures that weigh enough to be thrown and drag the line along behind them as they go. In fly-fishing, you are casting the weight of the line instead. Fly lines are thicker than other fishing lines, thick enough to be worked back and forth through the air on the same principle as a bullwhip. The fly is attached to a fine monofilament leader on the end of the line and simply goes along for the ride. Fly lines are usually plastic-coated and tapered on the end to improve the smoothness of the cast. It takes some practice to master this kind of casting, but to watch an accomplished caster working seventy feet of line on an eight-foot rod, to see the line looping and rolling straight out behind him, then, as he pushes the rod forward, to see the line roll cleanly out in front of him and settle gently across a stream, brings to mind more artful motions—ballet, perhaps—than are normally associated with fishing.

I spent my whole first summer fishing alone, in the privacy of my own home river, until I could push out a decent trout-fishing cast of forty feet and could catch Gardner fish with some regularity. It was only later that I even realized that some people could cast three times as far with less effort and learned how much there actually was to getting good at fly-fishing.

Learning to cast was only the beginning, and the least fun, of learning to fly-fish. Fly-fishing introduced me to the aquatic world I mentioned earlier and led me to look under countless rocks in the shallows for squiggly little marvels I never dreamed existed. It led me to learn to read water: to study a current and its behavior for what it could tell me about what lay beneath—where the insects, shelter, and fish might be found. In this it taught me to appreciate running, moving water and the constancy of its workings. For never did I visit this river without seeing something new, some slight change in the flow or in the cut of a channel or in the shape of a bank. The changes became part of the excitement for me, and each spring I eagerly awaited the passing of the snowmelt runoff, not only so that I could fish but also to see what new shapes the flow had taken in favorite spots. Over the years, some pools silted in while others deepened. A dislodged log would jam in a new position, and I would investigate it as the current dug a new trout shelter beneath it.

Most of this happened very slowly. A tree might be washed from its place on the bank by a sudden flood, or maybe it would be undermined gradually, as the water loosened the soil, bit by bit, finally persuading the tree to fall. If rivers were human, they would be very patient people.

Without fly-fishing I would never have gotten to know the dipper, a chubby gray bird of the West that is surely the cheeriest friend a fisherman could hope for. The dipper has puzzled many visitors; a ranger I know was once approached by a concerned visitor who reported seeing "a little gray bird commit suicide by walking right into a creek." The dipper, song-bird-shaped and a totally unaquatic-looking creature, lives on aquatic insects and small fish, chasing them under water without the benefit of webbed feet. Dippers build nests on low overhanging banks, right at the water, and spend their days splashing around in the shallows, frequently in very fast water (I've also seen them in lakes, where they may "fly" along right under the surface for several yards in pursuit of insects). They get their name not from their habit of taking an occasional "dip" in the water but from charming mannerism: As they jump from rock to rock, or sit surveying a likely current from shore, they do little bobbing knee-bends, one after another. At first it seems like a nervous twitch—something you hope they'll get over—but soon you get used to it and the dipper's little dance and shuffle become a special part of the day. Usually there is no more than one in sight, or maybe just a quick twittering warble as one flies by, but one winter when most of the river was rimmed with ice, I saw half a dozen at one time, each inspecting a different icy shelf along successive pools, a veritable platoon of bobbing, dipping, "fly"-fishers, attracted to the warm open water of the lower river. I suppose they compete with the trout for food, as they compete with me for trout, but it makes no sense to me to worry about such congenial competition. They and the trout have been living together for a long time, and I don't interfere all that much. Fishing depends a lot on such things as dippers, anyway.

But it depends as well on occasional success at catching fish. Success depends on many things, including skill, but especially luck. However, after you practice a lot you learn that more is involved than mere mechanical proficiency or good fortune, and that at times you expect to catch fish just because, well, you feel that you will.

For example, there are days when I feel especially in touch with the end of the line, when I feel every lift of the current, every tick of the hook on gravel, every tug of vagrant weed. Such a day was an evening in July, the most productive (of fish, anyway) I ever had on the Gardner.

I'd just read Sylvester Nemes' first book about "soft-hackle" flies, simple little wet flies without tails or wings: just slim bodies of fur or floss with a turn of partridge feather near the head. The partridge feather was marked with fine black lines that gave each individual barbule of fiber a segmented look; the barbules, in the water, responded to every wisp of current as the fly drifted along below the surface. Together, they flexed and wiggled like the legs on a struggling insect. Or so the theory ran; I can't know what the trout took them for, only that they took them. As more than one naturalist has pointed out, trout, having no hands, must examine curious objects with their mouths, whether they think they are food or are just amusing themselves to pass the time.

According to my stream log, the water this day was "gorgeous and low," and the angler was described as "a trifle low himself," though I don't recall why; the reason is probably better forgotten and surely was while fishing on this golden evening. As the shadow of Terrace Mountain climbed the slope of Mount Everts in front of me, the trout greeted the flies with embarrassing abandon. Each pool yielded its fish hastily; no sooner would I make my cast and begin to probe the suspected pockets and recesses of the opposite bank with the quivering fly when another rainbow would yank it, and me, from our thoughtful investigations.

By the time I reached the pool I most wanted to fish, I'd already released eight or ten small trout, up to ten inches, and was planning to throw away all my flies and replace them with hundreds of these magical soft hackles. This pool, a larger, broader version of most on the river, was about 60 feet across, and from where it was formed by a fast, bouncy riffle to where it broadened and fanned into an ankle-deep tail, it was perhaps 150 feet long. Along the east bank it was three to four feet deep, and the bank itself was undercut. It was one of the few pools on the river with that ominous darkness that says "big fish." Five years earlier I'd caught a fifteen-inch brown here on a grasshopper imitation, the first respectable brown I'd ever caught.

I squeezed a couple of small split-shot onto the leader about a foot above the fly (this practice is not recommended in the book I'd been reading, and many fly-fishers are offended by such a tactic as crass and unsporting, but I needed to work the fly deeply through this run, and I am generally unhampered by delicate sensitivities at such times) and waded into the shallows at the head of the pool. Remembering a lesson from another book, I pitched the fly slightly upstream of the pool, letting it sink as it washed from the riffle into the deep quiet water. I waited until it was moving slowly through the deep water, then, with a quick upward motion of the rod, I dragged it back to the surface. This, I'd read, imitated the upward motion of an emerging caddisfly. The fish must have thought so, and in an hour I doubled my total take, keeping a thirteen-and-a-half-inch brown for a late dinner. Unlike most pools on the river, this one occasionally yielded several fish from the same spot. Never before had it yielded fifteen as it did this night, but as long as they kept coming, I felt no urge to move on.

Toward dark I set the hook in a less yielding mouth and was met with firm resistance followed by a quick run that peeled a few yards of line from my reel. The fish didn't jump, but had the quickness of a rainbow (I have an unscientific approach to this; it felt like a rainbow). After a few minutes of short zigs and zags, parrying with the fish as I moved down to the shallow flat at the tail of the pool, I was able to pull it near enough to see. It was a big rainbow, fifteen or sixteen inches long and still quite strong. My leader was too light to simply horse the fish ashore, and I was in for several more minutes of fight when the fish turned into the current and fled downstream toward the next riffle, one of the few up here that I was afraid of—a vicious little roller coaster of jagged rocks and slippery footings, nowhere more than three feet deep but a guaranteed soaking for a clumsy wader. I held tight to the line as the fish swung below me and gained weight and speed in the quickening pull of the current. As soon as the line tightened directly downstream of me he broke off, taking the fly with him into the little rapid. I retrieved an empty line, with no regrets for once, pleased to have made the acquaintance, for the first time in five years, of the king of the pool.

These good-looking pools are usually not so generous. Another one, far downstream along the road to the North Entrance, frustrated me for a year or two. It was formed where a flat riffle broke over a bank and dropped into a hole the river had dug against the road embankment. I couldn't see the bottom of this one, and so I privately christened it the "salmon hole" because several huge fish could have hidden safely in the dark shadows under its broken surface.

I couldn't even figure out how to fish it. Approach from either side was by high banks where I was visible to the fish. As I climbed down to the stream I'd see smaller fish scatter from the shallows to the hole, presumably alerting whatever big fish lurked there. One evening I started in about a quarter mile above the hole, wading back and forth across the river between the deeper spots and catching just enough small fish to keep my interest up. I arrived at the riffle above the hole just about dusk. My normal approach was the standard approved one for fly-fishermen: I would try to cast up over the pool from below with a large floating fly. This time, however, unorthodoxy struck, and I crept through the weeds to a point near the upper end of the pool. The Gardner's fish aren't too particular about fly pattern; there's usually little need to imitate the prevailing insect activity precisely, so I rarely even think about such things. I had noticed, though, that on previous nights there were a good many large heavy-bodied crane flies in the air, flying just a few inches above the surface of the water, presumably mating. (Crane flies are those giant mosquitolike bugs that resemble flying daddy longlegs; their immature forms are usually aquatic, and the adults lay their eggs in quiet water.) I couldn't imagine any self-respecting fish not noticing these big guys, and so I rummaged through my fly boxes for a likely imitation. The one I found was a graceful monster fashioned by my brother some years earlier, of elk hair on a very long hook. It was well over an inch long altogether. Still crouched in the weeds, I fastened it to my leader and, somehow avoiding the high sage that waited to grab my backcast, I laid the line clear across the pool to the shallows near the far bank. Immediately the fast water in mid-pool dragged the line downstream, and the effect on the fly, on me, and on the fish, was electrifying. The fly floated quietly for an instant in the still water, and then, as the faster water hurried the long belly of line downstream, the fly was pulled out across the deeper water, skating hurriedly along on its light hackles and looking just like those big crane flies.

Its first such skating performance was uninterrupted but not, I was sure, unobserved. With a mild case of the shakes and a quickening pulse, I let the line drift completely down, then, still crouched, I lifted it into a low backcast and again tossed it across the pool.

Again the line bellied and doubled in the fast current. Again the fly rested only a second, then began its quick skittering over the deep water. But it had moved only a couple of yards when a big brown trout shot from the pool near it and took the fly in a smooth downward motion. Too surprised at that moment to consider this attack, I later realized how rarely it happens; fish usually just stick their heads up to the surface and inhale whatever is floating there, but this fish actually jumped high and clear of the water and took the fly on his way down, as he reentered the water nose-first. Perhaps prior experience with the crane flies had taught it that they escape if approached from underneath, or perhaps it just got so excited it missed the fly on the way up and lucked out and got it on the way down. With a power that surprised me, the fish bulled right up into the very point of the pool directly beneath the fastest water at its head. My leader was unusually light, so I had to play it gently, and I figured on gradually wearing the fish out as it fought both the current and my line. I hurried to the tail of the pool to keep well below it, but I must have pulled too hard, for it turned and raced past me into a stumbling riffle full of snags and small rocks. I somehow managed to lead it past the worst snags to a grassy bank in the quieter water below, where I foolishly dragged it up onto the shore just as the fly fell from its mouth (again, this happens often in fishing books, but of the thousands of trout I've caught this is the only time it's happened to me). It was a little more than fourteen inches long, a fine fat resident brown, and a fish I probably shouldn't have removed from the gene pool but did.

The brown trout came to North America in the early 1880s from the United Kingdom and Europe. It had reached the Yellowstone Plateau by about 1890, where it quickly helped other nonnative trouts replace the local cutthroat trouts and grayling. One reason this happened is that browns are a lot harder to catch than cutthroats and therefore withstand fishing pressure much better. A preliminary study done in the 1970s in ponds near the park showed that there, at least, cutthroats are sixteen times as easy to catch as browns (brook trout, known for gullibility, were only nine times as easy to catch as browns). People who have reason to think about such things wonder if cutthroats would be as easy to catch as they are if they, like the browns, had been fished over by savvy anglers with fine tackle for a couple millenia. What must such predation do to the genetic makeup of a fish population, having the easiest caught individuals removed from hundreds of generations?

But the browns, as hard as they are to catch that first time, are harder than hell to catch again. I learned that on my home river. A tiny step-across tributary ran past my quarters, bordering the lawn and then dipping into a sage field for maybe fifty yards before swinging behind a neighbor's lawn, where it widened into a small weed-filled pond. The water was partly runoff from the hot springs, so it was mineral-rich and supported heavy vegetation and lots of insect life. Brown trout were there, apparently remnants from hatchery ponds that had once sat nearby and had been fed by the creek. The pond was fished only by a couple of neighborhood kids who rarely caught anything, and the neighborhood osprey, who rarely put anything back. And me, for a few weeks one summer.

There was a narrow channel about 3 feet wide through the weeds, then the pond itself, about 40 feet wide and 3 feet deep at the most. The whole stretch ran no more than 120 feet, the length of one backyard. The trout rose easily to insects in the quiet water of the channel and the pond, and I could see them clearly, holding there within short casting distance. On hot bright days they all settled into a slightly deeper depression in the middle of the pond. From a hillock that bordered the yard I could see them holding there, in two rows. There seemed to be about fifteen of them.

I started fishing this stretch one evening after work. It was very civilized, standing on the comfortable lawn and dropping a wiggly little wet fly in front of each trout and snaking them out across the weedbeds as soon as they were hooked. I quickly measured each fish, clipped off a portion of the adipose fin (a harmless if insulting operation), and slid them back into the water. The first evening I caught five, measuring four to thirteen inches. The next night I caught five more, four to ten inches, and again clipped them all. The next night, two more. Five nights later, seven more. The afternoon after that I caught five more. The twenty-first fish I caught had a clipped fin; it was the thirteen-incher I'd caught the first day, a couple of weeks earlier. Over the next few weeks I caught a few more with clipped fins, but I'd learned a new respect for the brown trout. As informal as my little study had been, it had shown me what tough teachers the brown trout can be. I preferred easier.

A friend from Iowa, an enthusiastic outdoorsman, visited me one September. Because of an eccentric graduate chairman we had once taught under, we had adopted a formal manner of addressing each other, after our chairman's manner.

"Mr. Palmer, you must learn about fly-fishing. This isn't the Big Muddy, you know. We have trout here, not those disgusting mudfish you're so fond of catching."

"Mr. Schullery, if you can suppress your elitism about the Mississippi, I would like to learn about fly-fishing."

His first lesson was a few miles in the backcountry on the Lamar River, near the mouth of Calfee Creek. The upper Lamar contains many quick, unschooled cutthroat trout, easily caught most of the time. When we walked down to the river in front of the patrol cabin it was late afternoon but the sun was still bright on the water. It would not have looked, to an Iowa angler, like a very promising time to catch a fish.

"You sit down here on this rock, Mr. Palmer. I must find a grasshopper." I kicked through some nearby brush and quickly sorted an inch-long hopper from the leaves.

"Watch this closely, Mr. Palmer. It's important." I tossed the hopper into the stream about six feet from shore. It landed kicking, stirring up little ripples as it was washed along. It had floated only a few feet when it disappeared in a splashy blur of trout mouth, a small explosion of water that left Mr. Palmer wide-eyed. He was hooked. Within a few minutes I had him slapping a few feet of line out over the water, giving these unruly little cutthroats a chance at a bushy dry fly. One after another they poked their noses up under it, inhaled it, mouthed it thoughtfully for a second, then spit it out and sank back to shelter. Each time Mr. Palmer watched the whole rise, take, and rejection with a slack jaw and a slack line, never once trying to hook the fish.

"Mr. Palmer, you have to set the hook when they take the fly. Weren't you paying attention during the lecture?"

"Yes, Mr. Schullery, I understand. I saw you do it." He was earnest in the face of my exasperation.

"Well, then, Mr. Palmer, why didn't you set the damn hook?!"

"I never think of it at the time, Mr. Schullery. It's all so interesting to watch."

A few days later I took him to the upper Gardner. I led him to the bank and rigged up the rod as I continued my instruction.

"Now, Mr. Palmer, you should learn about where trout hold in the current." As I spoke I worked about twenty-five feet of line into the air, keeping it airborne above me, casting back and forth, ready to deliver. This was one of the few stretches of river I know of where what I was about to do was not the worst kind of reckless arrogance.

"They like water at the edges of the current, Mr. Palmer. See that rock there with the little eddy behind it, where the water is sort of still?" He was attentive, if skeptical, as I dropped a small dry fly into the spot, where it was instantly drowned but not eaten by one of the suicidal brook trout that inhabited this precious run. Mr. Palmer choked quietly as I whipped the fly back with a triumphant "Aha!" Then, as I dried it with some false casts, I remarked casually, "Look for calmer breaks in the current, Mr. Palmer, even if you can't see a rock or anything, like this one up here." I laid the fly onto a little slick in midstream, immediately grabbing it back from another splashy rise. This was not instruction; this was performance. Again and again I brought trout up, hooking a couple, missing most, reveling in the show they and I were putting on. And each time I'd raise a fish, Mr. Palmer, his voice a mixture of envy, respect, and disdain, would mumble, "Mr. Schullery, you bastard," or "This can't be. . ." I don't know how many fish I showed him in fifteen minutes, but it was many more than I'd imagined I would. The Gardner and its trout performed royally in beginning the education of yet another fly-fisherman.

A home river is that rarest of friends, the one who frequently surprises you with new elements of personality without ever seeming a stranger. The revelations are gifts, not shocks. Like Mr. Palmer, I seemed always to be discovering new secrets of the river; they weren't really secrets at all, just places waiting for me to become smart enough to notice them. It might be a new trout lie, hidden under a log and invisible from the trail I usually walked; a beaver dam that must be fished this season because it will be silted shallow by next; a deer bed in the willows behind a favorite pool; a deep pocket I never noticed until I walked the bank opposite the trail. What makes this so precious, like so many other meaningful pastimes, is the anticipation of revelations yet to come, or discoveries not fully understood, like the dark pool swarming with diptera that I discovered one day while searching for a drowning victim and never later returned to, off duty. Like the stretches of canyon water I never fished, that pool is a mystery and a promise, probably worth more in anticipation than it will be in actual sport.

Some revelations are bigger. In an isolated stretch of the upper river, where only brook trout were thought to reside, a pocket of rainbows was found, survivors of some long-forgotten stocking mission of several decades ago. They lived, unknown and unfished, in one short stretch of river, neither expanding their range into better traveled waters nor shrinking into oblivion. Further study may prove them to be of considerable scientific value. Like the other nonnative trouts in Yellowstone—brook, brown, and lake—they were placed here in the early days of fisheries science, before distinct strains of each species were hopelessly crossed and mixed in the great trout factories of modern hatcheries and in countless rivers where thoughtless and well-intentioned fisheries crews dumped new strains of trout on top of existing native populations. Yellowstone has waters, including my home river, that were stocked before that energetic "management" chaos mutilated our western trout taxonomy and were not stocked since; waters that now may give more than sport—they yield museum-pure strains of trout that we thought we'd lost.

It may not be easy for the non-fisherman to comprehend why such knowledge makes the fishing more exciting than it otherwise would be, but it is immensely satisfying to know such a thing. Fishing is a quest for knowledge and wonder as much as a pursuit of fish; it is as much an acquaintance with beavers, dippers, and other fishermen as it is the challenge of catching a trout. My home river does not always give me her fish, but the blessings of her company are always worth the trip.

Chapter Three

JUMPING WATER

THE SOFT inner walls of the canyon of the lower Gardner River, as often dried mudflow as sandstone, are constantly sloughing off, like some patient earthen glacier pouring slowly from the mountain above. The walls of the inner canyon are a cavalcade of gullies, gravel slides, and dirt piles. The jumble is so confusing that you can best appreciate what's happening—how the river keeps clearing the slipping debris from its path—from a distance.

Here and there in the canyon, harder crests of stone have been left jutting free from the receding dirt walls. One such prominence, Eagle Nest Rock, used to host an osprey pair; when I first started fishing the Gardner, what was left of their nest, weathered silver and battered apart, still topped the tower like an unruly wig. One day more than thirty years ago, while fishing in the canyon, I saw an osprey alight there as if checking out the neighborhood. For a moment I had hope that they'd return to the rock after many years of absence, but the bird rested only briefly, then flew away. I don't know why they don't return—I've heard they left years ago after a wrecked tank truck poisoned the fish in that stretch of river—but it could be heavier traffic than in earlier days or too many photographers. For whatever reason, the big nest remains an empty home.

Bighorn sheep move into the canyon in late fall, spending part of their time grazing up above in the open on McMinn Bench just east of the canyon, and the rest along the steep walls of the canyon itself. They stay there until early spring, some of the ewes not leaving until after lambing time.

So close to the road, so easily approached, these sheep seem almost unreal, even disappointing. More than any other North American grazer except the mountain goat, bighorns have a reputation for living in places only they can go. Hunters have been writing about the extraordinary challenge of sheep-hunting for more than a century. Having a band of bighorns walk in front of your car is great, but it also seems too easy. I want to object that sheep, like bears and other Yellowstone wildlife we desperately want to see, should be earned.

The canyon—indeed, the whole north end of the park in winter—attracts wildlife photographers in greater numbers than it attracts sheep. Stunning photographs with rugged, breathtaking backdrops can be had from a car window or, at best, an easy climb. I've seen any number of such photographs in magazines, recognizing the familiar background of north Yellowstone's scenery. The magazine's readers admire what difficulties must have been overcome to reach such a magnificent subject in such a wonderful setting. I've taken similar pictures, getting so close that through my zoom lens the nervously alert brown eyes of a restless ewe shamed me for disturbing these harassed gentle creatures.

Perhaps it's because the big animals are so easy to see when I live here, or maybe it's because I actually have become as open-minded about wildlife appreciation as I want to, but there are other, less glamorous animals that usually distract me from the sheep. For me, the center ring for the wildlife show in the canyon is down in the river and hardly anyone knows it. While the tourists and professional photographers line the roads watching the sheep, deer, and elk, I take myself to the slick rocks below a dark pool I know, lone witness to a silent miracle in the river.

The Gardner serves the Yellowstone River as a major nursery stream. Each fall Yellowstone River browns migrate up the Gardner and other feeders to spawn. Like so many miniature imitations of their salmon cousins, the browns crowd nervously from the depth, space, and security of the big river into the Gardner's shallow pools and riffles, returning, as near as we know, to the natal ground—to the very gravel beds from which they themselves were hatched years before.

I first encountered this spawning run on the closing day of trout season the first year I stayed in the park through the winter. I was fishing about a mile above the Gardner's mouth at the Yellowstone, working a weighted imitation stonefly nymph through a deep trough of slow water below a small cascade. The water was full of unhookable fish; they would strike savagely, but quickly slip from the hook before I could even identify them. I didn't know larger fish were in the river, had not imagined that the pool was any different from the week before, and hadn't yet noticed the faded clipping in the storehouse at Mammoth that showed the nine-pounder that Ed Wolfe had caught a few years earlier upstream from where I was.

So I was totally unprepared when on a long downstream swing my fly came to a stop in midcurrent. I had sense enough to set the hook, but there my involvement in the action ceased. A brown trout larger than any I had ever seen immediately had my attention.

During my brief attachment to this trout I learned much of practical value about the vigor, energy, and fabulous acrobatic abandon that the adult brown trout brings to its mating bed. Within ten seconds the fish was airborne—high arcing leaps—at least six times. It still seems impossible, as if it bounced from the surface of the water as from a trampoline rather than submerging and getting a good purchase on the water between each leap. It was not a true giant trout by local standards. I reckon it now, with the cooler eye of experience, at upwards of twenty inches, hardly three pounds. But in the confines of this small pool, the fish jumping insanely almost within reach of my rod tip, it was paralyzingly large. I was stunned and just watched.

Actually, even had I been clearheaded and prepared, there would have been nothing for me to do. According to the books, I should have been ready to "give line" from the reel, to fight the fish with the forgiving bend of the rod, to wear the fish out. None of this seemed to apply. The fish wanted no line; the thirty or so feet he had gave him ample freedom, especially as he chose to jump and run upstream, toward me. With him spending more time in the air than in the water, and hardly any time at all in any given place, it would have taken a much better angler than I to organize anything resembling a fight.

It didn't matter. On the last jump he threw the fly. The shattered surface of the pool ran out into the next run, washing my line ashore and leaving me giggling quietly.

A little checking around brought uneven information. Yes, this happens every year, but the run usually doesn't come in until after the season is closed, and some years there don't seem to be very many fish. No, it hasn't been studied much by the biologists but we do know that the Gardner is a damned important nursery for the Yellowstone browns. Yes, people catch big ones off the mouth of the Gardner, in the Yellowstone itself—look at those monsters hanging behind the bar down at the Town Cafe. Yes, locals do poach the devil out of the run sometimes. No, it isn't reliable enough to attract fishermen the way the runs on the Madison do; the fish aren't big or numerous enough even when the run does occur before the season closes. But it is kind of fun to go watch them jump in the cartwheel.

The cartwheel?

Yeah, you know, that chute of white water below that turn in the road in the canyon that gets bad when it's icy?

Yes?

Well, the trout have a hard time getting through that up to the spawning beds at Chinaman's Garden. They gather in that pool below the chute, everybody calls it the cartwheel, and every so often one will take a running start and pitch itself ass over teakettle into the fast water. Big long jumps.

I'm on my way.

For years, the stretch of river containing the cartwheel was closed to fishing well before the rest of the river, to protect early spawners and to foil meat fishermen who used sport gear to snag the vulnerable trout. Eventually, rocks shifted in the river bed and the fish no longer had to jump through the foam. The show was over. But every time I drive by, I still reflexively look down that way and remember those amazing jumpers, and I'm there again, and I remember how it was back then.

By the time the fish started coming in, that stretch of the river was without human visitors and I usually had the cartwheel to myself. I drove by and pulled over to where I could look down the bank to the white water. If I saw no jumpers in five minutes or so I didn't hang around. At peak times there may have been a jumper every twenty seconds, and if I saw one or two jump fairly quickly I'd stop the engine and climb down to the rocks.

At low water, in late fall, the cartwheel was mostly confined to a rock chute about twelve feet wide with large flat shelves right up to its edge. The shelves had an inch or two of water flowing across them, but practically the whole river was gathered above the chute in a rocky defile and pushed wildly into the narrow cut, where it churned and foamed down, more a torrent than a current. The chute emptied into a tight, deep hole of the darkest water on the river, stirred there momentarily, then plunged on down through a series of stair-step rapids. The Gardner in its canyon is a high-energy river.

The dark pool served as a staging area for upstream migrants. When the run was on, they gathered in this swirling little cauldron of rock, taking turns at the cartwheel. Sometimes, standing right at the brink of the rock ledge, I looked down and saw a big roiling ball of brown trout—dozens at least, ten to sixteen inches—being churned around like a tangled wad of earthworms in the quieter side of the pool. The ball seemed to drift in and out from the ledge, sometimes partly obscured by the bubbles and foam from the cartwheel, sometimes sinking deeper until it was lost to sight. From it came the jumpers.

On the West Coast, I've seen big salmon jumping; it's fast, but the size of the fish makes the process observably graceful. A thirty-pounder emerges from the water in a smooth arc, shedding water from its sides as it climbs into the air. Some jumps seem almost ponderous. Not so with the trout here in the cartwheel; all was flashing speed. One at a time, the trout got a short running start below the chute and emerged from the foam somewhere near the lower end. As they shot clear of the water, their tails often fluttered, too fast to see, as if they sought a hold on the air to match the one they used to launch themselves from the water. More disconcerting than the frenetically kicking tail was their seeming abandonment of normal orientation. They did go ass over teakettle, as if they were being thrown by someone: Here comes one sideways, spinning slowly, nose-over; Here's one upside down, followed by one curled like a horseshoe; Then, a traditionalist, in a classic headfirst leap as good as any jumper in a Winslow Homer watercolor.

Obviously, considering their flight plans, they landed with varying fortunes. The chute was fierce, and most seemed to be washed back down the instant they hit the upper end of it. In all my watching I never saw a fish make it, though I know some did. Some smacked wetly, still buzzing their tails, onto the rocks at the edge of the chute. (A biologist friend tells me that migrating trout in other places have been known to throw themselves against unpassable dams until their heads split open.) Others landed in the shallow racing sheets of water that covered the bordering ledges. When a fish found this water, truly furious swimming could carry the day, for the ledge lead along the side of the chute clear up to calmer water. Once, watching with a friend, we found ourselves cheering these ledge-swimmers on. We stood on dry rock only a couple of feet away, crouched over, yelling absurdly at a trout as it swam frantically in three inches of water (like a swimming coach running alongside the pool to exhort an athlete to keep pushing). When the trout gave up and was washed limply back into the chute, we would let out an "awww . . ." like fans watching a golf ball come to rest on the lip of the cup.

The admiration I'd gained from hooking one of these trout was nothing compared to what I came to feel at the jumping water. If I ever in my life show such intense single-minded devotion to a goal, even one as simple as procreation, I will die satisfied. The trout simply *had* to move up. They had to get through the cartwheel.

What makes this most wondrous is where they were going: the very gravel bed they, each individual to its own, had hatched from years before. In early winter I'd make my way to two or three favored spots on the river, choosing a fairly windless day if I could (it's hard to see through a ruffled surface). Watching some of the larger gravel bars, where the water was only a foot or two deep, I might count thirty fish finning quietly or jockeying for position: osprey heaven. Light spots would appear on the gravel—oblongs two feet in length—where females had dug shallow depressions, or redds, by turning sideways and rapidly fanning the dirt and stones out with their tails. Eventually, with one or more males in attendance, the female laid her eggs into the depression, the male ejecting his milt in a fine settling fog at the same time. The process would be repeated until the females were out of eggs, and after a while the trout would drift back down to the bigger river, leaving behind only the resident trout who would dine heartily on the hatchlings (their own included) a few weeks later.

In 1983, my friend John Varley and I wrote a book about Yellowstone's fish. The book was something of equal-rights statement for fish, in which we tried to get people to think of fish as wild animals—as wildlife. Our point was that it's too bad that more people don't open up to the excitement of the aquatic wilderness; it's a great show and you don't have to fish to enjoy it. Even in hard winter, with no thoughts of fishing, I often find myself drawn to the river.

In fact, even when the spawners have left the beds and only an occasional fish is to be seen, and when the cliffs are crawling with bighorns and the willow with deer, my attention keeps coming back to those dark currents whose ephemeral inhabitants overcome objects like none I can imagine facing. I drive to a parking place I know and walk the paths a little more, and as I head back to the car, kicking through drifts where in summer I would be hip-deep in sage, and as I drive back up to my place at park headquarters, I watch the water at every opportunity. Over the years I've learned every spot on the road that gives me a glimpse of the river and how long I dare take my eyes from the road at each one. Like the satisfaction of looking at a mountain range that you know has grizzly bears, there is much to be said for a good look at a wild river, and I always look with special joy at the jumping water, even when the foam is empty of trout.

Chapter Four

ANTLERS AWEIGH

ONE COLD, wet evening almost forty years ago, I was fishing the Au Sable in Michigan. The river was in flood and the fishing was lousy, but even then I had grasped the wisdom that was just becoming popular on bumper stickers, that "poor fishing is better than any kind of work." I had stayed a little too late, and it was a little too dark, and I was just about to wade out to shore, having also grasped the wisdom that poor fishing in the dark in a flooded river is better than any other kind of suicide. I was at that point where I had made my last cast of the night for about the tenth time when I noticed something bobbing along in midcurrent upstream at the next bend.

This was fairly big water, some miles downstream from Mio, where a whole tree could be hauled along by the river, so my first thought was that this was probably a sunken log with some funny snags sticking up. But it soon resolved itself into the head and upper neck of an antlerless deer, which I assumed was a doe. She was swimming along with the current, the rhythmic pulling of her front legs evident in the rise and fall of her head. Standing there in fairly shallow water with the solid forest behind me, I was invisible to the deer so I watched her until she was almost even with me, out in the middle of the river.

As she approached, my curiosity got the best of me and I had to know just how much control she had over her course. This was back in fiberglass days, and I had been dredging big streamers with a powerful Fenwick ten-weight nine-foot rod that my brother sarcastically referred to as "the barge pole." I slapped it down on the river in front of me a couple times, and the doe reacted instantly. She made a hard right turn and, with surprising disregard for the river's powerful current, swam straight to the opposite bank. As soon as she was out of the water on the bank, she paused for a moment, looked back toward the source of the sound, then disappeared into the trees. I don't think she ever saw me.

My first thought was that something had probably chased her into the water. About that time I also did a little deer hunting (not to be confused with actual deer shooting) in Michigan, and learned that there was an intense local tradition among local hunters, of hatred of loose dogs in the woods, for this very reason. But then, thinking it over a little more and remembering her obvious familiarity and comfort in the water, it occurred to me that perhaps she was simply going somewhere by the quickest possible route, and perhaps it wasn't a dumb dog but a dumb fisherman who was the only interruption of her evening.

Deer are, indeed, confident swimmers. Most of what exists in the written record on this subject is scattered widely but generously in the older sporting literature, that terrible-but-wonderful body of first-hand recollection and instruction that until the last few decades was often the best published source of natural history information that we had on many subjects. Sportsmen in nineteenth-century America frequently wrote about deer swimming across lakes in popular recreation areas such as the Adirondacks. One of the many debates over sporting ethics (or the lack thereof) in those days involved the killing of swimming deer. By the early 1900s, it was pretty much agreed, at least among the conservation-minded sportsmen, that only a lout or a moron would shoot a swimming deer or employ the other common tactic of paddling alongside the deer in a canoe, cutting the deer's throat, and towing it ashore.

There were also non-hunting accounts in the outdoor press. In 1896, *Forest and Stream*, a great repository of all sorts of sporting instruction and nature lore, reported that a deer had been sighted more than a mile off the Rhode Island coast, industriously swimming out to sea. Other deer in other contemporary accounts were seen as much as five miles from shore in both the Atlantic and Pacific Oceans. Ernest Thompson Seton, the famous early-twentieth-century nature writer, gathered up several such accounts and concluded that deer are "so confident of their swimming powers that they invariably make for the water when hunted to extremity. There are many many cases on record of deer so pushed, boldly striking out into the open sea, trusting to luck to find another shore."

No doubt many deer developed this habit from moving between islands and mainland, whether along the Inside Passage of the Canadian coast, the labyrinth of lakes and islands of the Canadian/ United States boundary waters, or any other place where deer range is divided by water. The famous little deer of the Florida Keys are known to swim from key to key, movements that are apparently important to that strain of deer's genetic well-being because it allows the small herds on various keys to mix now and then. Early one morning on No-Name Key (I'm not being coy; that really was its name), driving down a dead-end road to a recommended fishing spot, I saw one cross in front of me. It was no bigger than a small dog. Something that size churning along over the deep channels between keys must at least occasionally provoke a spectacular rise from a big shark.

The primary interest in all this for fishermen lies in deer hair. Deer hair is among the most popular natural materials for making lures and flies, a trick that many early American anglers probably learned from Native Americans. In the early 1800s in the Great Lakes, they were observed trolling from canoes using an entire white-tailed deer tail with hooks in it to catch muskies, pike, and other large freshwater fish.

Deer hair played prominently in one origin story of largemouth bass fishing. The pioneering naturalist William Bartram, on his famous collecting trip through the American Southeast in 1774, saw local people fishing with a "bob," a large treble hook around which was wrapped a sizeable portion of a deer tail, red cloth, and colored feathers. Bartram said the resulting lure was "nearly as large as a fist." The bob was tied to a line about two feet long on the end of a twelve-foot pole. As one man quietly paddled the boat along a shore, the other stood in the bow and waved the bob around just over the surface of the water near weed beds. The explosive strike of a ten- or fifteen-pound largemouth bass as it rushed from the cover of lily pads to take the bob must have been as exciting sport as any had by the most overtackled present-day angler.

Modern "bucktail" flies resulted from the availability and versatility of deer tails, whose fine, long hairs make excellent and lively imitations of small fish. But bucktail is not the hair of greatest interest to me, either as a fisherman or as a naturalist. The body hair is, for the same reason it is important to the swimming deer: it floats really well. Deer body hair contains countless air cells (it is sometimes described as "hollow," but it doesn't have an empty core, just lots of tiny air cells). Fly tiers notice this the first time they lash a bundle of deer hair down onto the shank of a hook; the thread just tightens and tightens until the hair under the thread is compressed quite flat while its loose ends splay widely. It's one of those unforgettable early revelations for the new fly tier, like the first time you see a hackle wrapped on a hook and watch that wonderful 360-degree circle of fibers make a neat collar around the hook. Elk, moose, pronghorn, and even mountain goat hair has been similarly employed, of course, and specialists long ago recognized and exploited advantages in the hairs from different parts of the animals' bodies and legs.

Deer molt twice a year, wearing a light summer coat for five or so months and a heavier winter coat the rest of the time. Those same nineteenth-century hunters who wiped out the Eastern Whitetail in much of its range said that if you shot or knifed a swimming whitetail that was wearing its "red" summer coat, someone better have a really good grip on its tail or antlers or it would just sink out of sight. But if it was killed in its "blue" winter coat it would probably float for a while. The winter coat, being thicker, held more air both inside each fiber and trapped between them (it didn't hurt that the deer had been fattening up for winter; that extra layer of fat also helped keep it afloat). The doe I saw in the Au Sable that evening was probably almost rid of her winter coat. Swimming was serious work for her.

All my readings about deer in water had described deer who were just traveling across water to get to the other side or trying to escape some pursuer. But that night my deer was clearly doing more than this, taking a ride in the current for whatever reason. Perhaps she used the river routinely to get from one part of her range to another. I would trade all the painstakingly made little deer-hair flies in my fishing vest for another chance to watch her go by. This time I wouldn't spook her. I'd let her pass, and then, if I could jog along in the dusk as fast as she could swim, maybe I could follow her far enough to learn her destination.

Chapter Five

RIVERS IN EXILE

NOW THAT I live in the Rockies all the time, I suppose I've gotten a little complacent about it somehow being a life I'm entitled to. But when I started, it was something that I struggled to maintain and that I regularly had to abandon for extended stretches of time. Most often, those stretches involved periods of unemployment or graduate school, when I would return to my parents' place in a southern Ohio town of about 35,000 people (a "town" in Ohio that is: it would be a city in Wyoming or Montana). Generous, good-humored, and endlessly patient people, my parents put me up while I finished a quarter of school, or crammed for some required-skill examination, or just waited until I could get back to Wyoming. The food, the housing, and the emotional support were all anyone could ever hope for, but I missed the wild country almost beyond endurance. A few times I escaped to fish Michigan's trout streams with my brother, but mostly I just moped along waiting for it to be over.

My restlessness drove me out on endless walks, and it didn't take me long to find my way to a small creek that trickled through a high-banked ditch along one edge of a small public park just a few blocks from my parents' house. Once I noticed it, I often went back, and began to count on it.

Water is always more or less wild. We pen it up behind dams, we run it through pipes, we spread it over fields, we slosh it around in bathtubs and swimming pools and tea kettles, but water always obeys the same fundamental physical laws. Most of all, it obeys gravity. Even when appearing motionless, the water is responding to gravity—pushing against what contains it, piling up on what is beneath it, and always storing energy that can do all sorts of extraordinary things if it is ever released. And, unlike living organisms, water does not have to exercise patience. It just sits there. But the instant it is free, it quite literally goes wild. No delay, no fanfare, just motion.

This little creek in my neighborhood was that way. Though imprisoned by high banks and cluttered with shopping carts, rubber sandals, hamburger wrappers, and less savory urban litter, it had no choice. And, in late winter and early spring, when low flows left most of its ditch bed dry, the water expressed its loyalty to gravity in a wonderfully visible way. In a process whose actual details professional hydrologists apparently still argue over, the creek began to meander.

To my sight, the creek's path of least resistance might have been a straight shot down the middle of the flat bed of the ditch. To the creek, the bed of the ditch was not flat, but a microcosm of the broad lowland valleys of countless rivers on the planet, where the water responds to subtle contours, changes in soil density, and other influences, finally becoming the classic meandering river so celebrated in song, art, and the souls of anglers and other river addicts everywhere. Here in this little ditch, though I couldn't see them, there were so many irregularities and inconsistencies in and under the soil that the creek was bound to deviate from a straight line. And, once that process began—perhaps it only took the stream entering that stretch of straight ditch at an odd angle to set up the action—the creek became what wild water virtually always becomes, given the chance. It became a winding river, only a few feet wide but possessed of all the independence of motion its tiny bed could accommodate.

Of course once it achieved that, it had me. Winding rivers, like roads stretching to remote horizons, are archetypal images that we respond to on deep and murky levels. They beckon us. They beg to be followed. They make the big promise, the one with no clarity but all the power in the world. Snowmelt running off a slope, car-wash water running down a driveway, rain in a street gutter—they're all the same to me. As soon as water gets rolling and starts its show, I just have to stop for a minute and watch.

Rivers typically meander at rates and dimensions that are roughly predictable. The "wavelength" of the meander, which one authority defines as "the straight-line distance across one complete S of the winding course," is typically about eleven times the size of the river's channel. This is said to hold true no matter what the size of the stream, and my extremely casual observations don't give me any reason to doubt it. Having eyeballed streams from the tiniest trickle fresh from a subalpine seep to huge lowland rivers, I'd have to say this sounds like an entirely plausible generalization. Certainly my town creek was up to something on about that scale, interrupted by the occasional bald tire or cinder block that, like some immense hard-rock obstruction in a free-running Montana trout stream, sent the creek careening off in a different direction and launching a whole new set of meanders.

What makes all this so wondrous is that though the general pattern of a stream's course is predictable, the individual variation is endless. I know what will happen; I just don't know what it will mean this time. Like listening to yet another performance of a familiar Bach piece, or tasting yet another interpretation of a hot fudge sundae, or further exploring any great relationship you may have with any person, place, or thing—each new encounter only enriches the acquaintance. There are always surprises.

It seems odd, but perhaps makes a kind of perverse sense, that it took a creek as abused and destitute as this one to help me realize why moving water is so magical. Stripped of all the easy thrills—ecological health, spectacular surroundings, charismatic fauna—this little creek had nothing left to show me but fundamentals. Without the usual distractions of biology, landscape, and rising trout, I could appreciate those fundamentals for all their glory.

Standing on the Main Street bridge, or walking along the banks, I somehow found great comfort in the little creek's attempted restoration of wildness, the irresistibility of its loyalty to fluvial process. Without succumbing entirely to fantasy, I could look at this tiny flow of water and make some happily familiar equations. The inside bends of some of the better established meanders—these would be long, arcing gravel bars on a western trout stream—were sprouting new grass and weeds, the equivalent of the willows and even cottonwoods I might expect on the bigger thing. Tiny cutbanks appeared along outer bends, again familiar except for scale. I could see the pool-and-riffle pattern of larger streams, the repeating, predictable pattern of shallow and deep water that is described as "vertical meanders"—the streambed goes up and down just as it moves from side to side. It was all there, and sometimes I involuntarily looked for the "good places," the ones that, if the creek were thirty feet wide instead of thirty inches, would hold fish. I tell you that I found more comfort in this than I would have thought possible, and that I didn't dare think about it too long or I'd get more homesick than was seemly.

Upstream from the Main Street bridge, past the aging Burger Chef and the Kroger's parking lot and on up behind the hospital, the creek emerged from its own little forest. This reach, though still safely contained in higher banks, had been allowed more flexibility. It had time to entrench its meanders into permanence and, with the help of the cover and heavier bankside vegetation, to get back into the business of harboring life. One day in a relatively sheltered bend (by "relatively," I only mean fairly free of burger wrappers and cardboard boxes) my angler's search image unexpectedly locked onto the familiar shapes of several small fish. I had no idea what species they were—some kind of minnow, I supposed. They were elongated, had some indistinct lateral striping, and reminded me vaguely of perch, which I was sure they were not. There was one larger one, perhaps ten inches long, and three or four little ones "attending" it. They all held and swayed in their little run, barely covered by the water. They never seemed to notice me, standing there a little ways back from the bank, looking at them like they were a twenty-dollar bill on the sidewalk.

I suspected that the big one was a female and the smaller ones were males interested in spawning. I wondered if they lived in some deeper stretch but came up into this shallow run to spawn. I developed scenarios for their lives, which was somehow more satisfying than going to the library and looking them up.

Most of all, I wondered over all the endless miles of unattended streams in this region where fish like these—so many species, some native and some not—went about their routines and rituals with even less regard for us than we have for them. Lacking the size and caché and pretty spots and literary celebrations and red stripes and preferred feeding habits that attract sportsmen or any other constituency, these fish were entirely without human justification, and except when we felt obliged to wipe out their kind to make room for some species we could enjoy more easily, their generations slipped by with all the anonymity and ease of some goggle-faced creature bumbling around a geothermal vent six miles deep in the ocean. They barely existed in our minds, and yet the sight of them that day was a great relief to me.

It has been many years since I've done much exile time, but I have never forgotten those fish. I have often imagined them and all their sluggish-water kindred, quietly going about their evolutionary business in a million undistinguished little runs and pools—dodging beer cans and backhoes, succumbing to sudden washes of pollution when some moron changes his oil upstream, slowly recolonizing their benighted realms, and all the while sustaining just a faint trace of wildness in a hard-used place. That memory mostly serves to sustain the gratitude that I still feel to them, and to their little river, for helping me get along in exile. But I suspect it has also elevated my awareness of the beauty of wildness wherever it happens, whether it attracts fly fishers, nature lovers, and others of our ilk who tend too often to seek the easy thrill of remote wildness and to neglect the wildness close at hand.

Chapter Six

CAIRNS POOL REVELATIONS

IN 1978, not long after moving from Yellowstone to Vermont to become director of what was then called the Museum of American Fly Fishing and is now known as the American Museum of Fly Fishing, I needed to attend the regional conclave of what was then called the Federation of Fly Fisherman but is now called the Federation of Fly Fishers. My friends from Orvis (which is stll called Orvis), John Harder and Bill Cass, found space in their van-full of Orvis displays and fishing tackle goodies for the museum's traveling exhibits, and we drove down to Roscoe, New York, in the Catskills.

It was early June, time for one of the great eastern mayfly hatches, the Green Drake and its extraordinary spinner, known locally as the Coffin Fly. During the next day, as we tended our respective exhibits at the conclave, Bill occupied himself and charmed the crowd by tying elegant porcupine-quill, extended-body imitations of the Coffin Fly in happy anticipation of the evening's fishing.

Fresh from the West, I mentally inventoried the obese Humpies, Sofa Pillows, other ill-mannered western flies in my vest. I could think of nothing that even faintly resembled either Bill's flies or the actual insects, a few of which I'd gotten a good look at the night before during a hasty stop for a few casts on the Willowemoc.

Besides, having read so much about these historic streams, and having absorbed the fly-fishing culture's reverence for them, it was hard to imagine pitching a Humpy into such famed pools and runs. Even today, having long escaped the worst effects of the Eastern Angling Establishment's history myths while retaining a broader admiration for their glorious traditions, it still feels like there would be something disrespectful—an almost flatulent rudeness—in using such flies in such a place.

That evening we adjourned to the river, specifically Cairns Pool, where we met a couple New York friends. We waded over toward the far bank, lined up about thirty feet apart, and began casting to nothing in particular. I was at the downstream end of the line, intimidated by the obvious skills of my companions and a little awed by the immense amount of angling folklore and tradition that ran through this valley.

When the fish didn't materialize, we resorted to the angler's most reliable fallback: cynical humor and pointed remarks about each others' casting skills. But just at dusk the first spinner appeared, looking like some bizarre little black and white helicopter humming low over the water. Soon the trout, who had obviously been waiting just as impatiently as we had, began to suck the big flies under. Our casting became more determined, even a little frantic.

The trout were having none of it. They eagerly took the naturals and ignored all the beautiful flies my friends expertly cast over them, flies that looked exactly like the real thing, as far as I could tell from casting distance. For half an hour or so, as the spinner fall grew into a full-blown biological spectacle, five college-educated men were made fools of by an unspecified number of small, intellectually challenged animals that didn't even have opposable thumbs.

At last, my self-training on western rivers asserted itself and I started thinking—not about tradition but about what I was actually seeing. These were big, long-bodied insects that seemed to lie flat on the water. Something was wrong with the finely constructed, beautiful imitations. Did I have any flies that did justice to any part of a real Coffin Fly? Rooting around in the grimier corners of my vest, I found a clumsily tied muddler-like grasshopper whose meaty yarn body appealed to the western cousins of these fish. I tied it on, threw it out there, and immediately had the evening's first strike.

It was with considerable and understandable pride that I heard the word "Hopper!" echo excitedly down the row of fishermen, as they all dug through their Wheatleys in search of such a sacrilegious, improbable thing. John quickly hooked a heavy trout—mine proved to be just a tiddler—on a Letort Hopper, and he used up most of the remaining light controlling its wallowing fight. We still didn't catch many, but at least we didn't get skunked.

I've devoted big parts of several books to the mystery of the fly and our inexhaustible enthusiasm for making sense of the trout's contempt for most of what we cast to them. In all that thinking and writing I have rarely come to a conclusion—at least not the sort of conclusion that will make the flies I tie and buy work any better. I enjoy fly fishing at least as much for all the daft and quirky things that happen—its vast capacity for improbabilities—as for its more widely advertised pleasures. I can't speak for anyone else, but irony, humor, and downright weirdness have always featured prominently in my fishing life, and my reading of the sport's history suggests that they've always been more common than our traditional chronicles have allowed. That evening on the Beaverkill, there on some of the most hallowed water in American fly fishing's shrine-dense land-scape, with masterful casters and expert fly tiers all around me, the trout once again reminded me that, despite all our notions and pre-tensions, they're still in charge, and we still don't get it.

Part Two:
Trout Weirdness

Chapter Seven

A LOT OF STRANGE STUFF

We once, when angling with the minnow in Leader Water, caught a trout of five or six ounces in weight with the tail of a fish protruding about an inch from its mouth, on pulling out which we found it to be a trout in a partially digested state, which, when its neighbor swallowed it, must have weighed at least two ounces. This did not prevent it from rising at the minnow, but its mouth being so full it could not get hold of it, and it was only after repeated rises that it was caught by the outside of the mouth.

William Stewart, *The Practical Angler* (1857)

ABOUT THIRTY years ago, Datus Proper and I struck up a correspondence and friendship, but I don't remember why. It was probably about the time I reviewed his thoughtful book *What the Trout Said* (1982) for *Rod & Reel*, but it may just have been that we had enough in common that eventually we had to talk about it.

Perhaps the most important thing we shared was serious Yellowstone history. Datus spent much of his boyhood there in the 1940s and 1950s, where he learned to fly fish from one of the park's most renowned rangers, Scotty Chapman.

With that pedigree and his great observational gifts, it's no wonder that Datus had many things to say that were of interest to me, and one of the best things he said was that I should fish his creek. He lived in Virginia at the time, just wrapping up a long career with the Foreign Service that had enabled him to fish some of the world's most interesting trout streams. As he approached retirement but still lived in Virginia, he acquired part interest in a stretch of one of the Gallatin Valley's wonderful spring creeks. By this time, I had left Vermont and returned to the West. I lived in Livingston, Montana, only about an hour from his creek, and he encouraged me to fish it now and then, on the condition that I report to him on how the water was.

That's how it happened that one bright, still day in early July 1985, my then-wife, Dianne Russell, and I were on Datus's creek, the best possible place to suffer the 100-degree heat. Maybe I should have known that it was liable to be a weird sort of day, because our best fish of the day, a heavy sixteen and a half inch brown that Dianne took on a number twenty poly-wing spinner, was and still is still the only fish I've ever seen jump out of the water onto the bank, then jump back in the water.

But that was only the warmup act for strangeness to come, which I described to Datus in a letter:

> You might think I'm not properly plugged in if I tell you this, but you're the only other person who might recognize it, so I'll tell you anyway. On two or three occasions, when a fish swam past me very fast after having been spooked upstream (or just because he was going somewhere), I think I *heard* him. There was a fluttering noise, almost like the wings of a small bird, and it only occurred those few times fish went past. They were swimming very fast, and their tails were really going. Have you ever heard that? I don't remember ever hearing it before and the first time I heard it I didn't really make the connection between the noise and the trout. After a couple times I realized what it was.

Or what I thought it was, anyway.

Datus didn't have much to say about it, and I didn't mention it to anyone else. It was just a little too bizarre for common consumption, so I filed it away in my growing "trout weirdness" memory file. On the one hand, I agree with old Henry Van Dyke, who, in *Fisherman's Luck* (1899), said that the great things about fishing were "the enchantment of uncertainty," and "tempting the unknown with a fishing-line," and escaping "from the tedious realm of the definite." On the other hand, some of the things we run into out there are just a little too uncertain, unknown, and indefinite to expect anyone but an eyewitness to believe.

Creepy Water

But they happen to all of us, and once in a while we get bold enough to try to tell others. Once in an even rarer while, others may believe us. In *Trout Madness* (1960), Robert Traver shared such an experience:

> Over a long period of years I have observed a certain strange fishing phenomenon—and one that I have yet to see mentioned or even hinted at in all the scores of fishing treatises and assorted revelations I have read. It is this: On some days the surface of the water possesses a peculiar gun-metal sheen, a kind of bland, polished, and impersonal glitter, a most curious sort of bulging look, coupled with the aloof, metallic quality and cold, glassy expression of a dowager staring down a peasant through her lorgnette. At the same time there is a deceitful appearance of warmth, an opaque expression of bland geniality, and the light reflects off the water in a curiously false-friendly way. It is all very subtle and confusing and hard to describe, yet when I see it I never for an instant mistake it. On such days, fortunately rare, I have learned that I might just as well leave my rod in the case and instead go chase butterflies or lurking girl-scout leaders.

I had only been fishing for a few years when I read this, but I knew exactly what he meant. Some of the Wyoming streams where I did most of my fishing and learning in those days could be just like that. As Traver said, it didn't happen often, but when it did it was unmistakable. And it was a sure guarantee of lousy fishing.

Like Traver, I couldn't imagine the cause of the mysterious quality of light and reflection he described. One would think that water can only reflect the sky in so many ways, and that those reflections can only have so many effects on the fishing. Apparently it isn't that simple.

But I didn't get all of the impressions that Traver got. I had seen water with just the appearance he described (though I have never personally observed a dowager, with or without a lorgnette). But for me there was nothing "false-friendly" about it at all; it was downright ominous, right from the start. The sheen of dead-gray opaqueness made the surface of the stream seem all but impenetrable, as if it wouldn't even allow a fly to sink. It was that unpleasant. I can only echo Traver's relief that it doesn't happen often.

Eventually I learned that weird water can happen for several reasons. Yellowstone's famous 1988 fires caused some of the most interesting water I've ever seen. In the summer of 1989, as spring runoff flushed a lot loose soil and burned matter off the landscape into the streams, my same local river would take on a peculiar dark lustre. The more sensationalist commentators were fond of declaring that "the rivers ran black," but that seemed to me a simplistic description of the actual tint, which was indeed quite dark but never, to my eyes at least, achieved blackness. What it achieved instead was a kind of slate grayishness, a sort of non-color with an odd glint that made me feel like I wasn't really casting into water at all, but into some other substance of a more alien and ethereal nature.

A lot of local fishermen, and even more tourist fishermen, were alarmed by this funny-looking water, and there were predictable and absurb proclamations of doom for the trout population. As it turned out, for some complicated set of reasons angler catch rates and fish sizes actually increased slightly that first year after the fires. Besides the rare opportunity to watch my favorite river deal with the complex ecological jolt of a partially burnt watershed, I got in on some bizarre fishing conditions. To fish a river for many years and then suddenly see it so subtly and intriguingly transformed by its own ecological development was all gain.

Besides, a pal of mine from Pennsylvania who I took to fish the stream when it was in full flush with this dark water said that it made his dry flies really easy to see even if he didn't catch anything.

I had a much less uplifting if no less strange a time on a small creek in the Yukon some years later. Its name was Moose Creek, and for the most part there was nothing to distinguish it from innumerable other Moose Creeks in the far north except that it was spooky.

Moose Creek was about twenty feet wide and mostly just a few inches deep. It flowed evenly but sluggishly along the base of a nearly thirty-foot bank. It looked like it should stink at little, but it didn't. Trees on both sides overhung and enclosed the stream, but they were high enough to allow fly casting as long as I cast directly up- or downstream. I got to the water about 8:30 in the evening with several hours of dim but useful northern summer light still available. It was hot, there were a lot of mosquitoes, and as far as I could see there weren't even any deep spots for fish to hide in, but to that point in my trip local advice had been batting about .500, which was pretty good by my standards, so I stuck with it.

I made some nice casts through the high tunnel of trees and alders that were hanging down on both sides. I accurately, even gracefully (not my normal adverb), put a #16 Adams into a number of likely spots. The wading couldn't have been easier.

But the whole place, the whole mood of the evening, felt wrong. The slow current was unable to prevent the buildup of algae on the fine gravel bottom of the stream, whose color most closely resembled the deep near-black of a heavily tinted windshield. The thin northern light filtered weakly through the forest canopy in an ominous funereal dusk. Nothing stirred; even the mosquitoes seemed depressed. Every cast felt somehow unwelcome, as if the stream would rather the line didn't land on it, thank you. After half an hour or so, this increasingly oppressive atmosphere brought on one of those hackle-stirring moments when senses you usually don't think you even have, senses that operate well below the conscious level, forcefully assert themselves and put you in the sort of subdued near-panic that you'd have to be an idiot to ignore. So I left.

A Lot of Strange Stuff

There's a deathless if little celebrated moment in the movie *Star Wars: A New Hope*, when Luke Skywalker asks Han Solo if he believes in The Force. Han didn't, but the first part of his answer to Luke is perhaps my favorite line in the whole six-episode *Star Wars* extravaganza: "Kid, I've been from one end of this galaxy to the other, and I've seen a lot of strange stuff . . ." What a wonderful description of a full life.

Something like this happens with fishing. Put in enough time, even if you never travel far, and you're bound to see some strange stuff, even if you're reluctant to tell your friends about it.

The popular Pennsylvania outdoor writer Charles Fox had the luxury of telling such a story and knowing it was irrefutable. In *This Wonderful World of Trout* (1963), Fox told of being invited to fish on a private pond, freshly stocked with 250 trout, as part of a local television show. The director, not a fisherman, was clueless of how hard it can be to catch a fish on demand, but as the cameras rolled and Fox prepared to cast, everyone noticed that the largest trout, a big brown, for some reason had a large red-and-white Daredevle spoon hanging from its dorsal fin. The director immediately decided that this was the fish Fox must catch.

Fox hopelessly cast toward it, and as his small barbless dry fly hit the water, "about half a dozen wakes converged upon it and the fly disappeared in a boil." Fox set the hook, and after things settled down and the fish could be seen, Fox and the film crew discovered that the fly had indeed found its way to the big fish, but was hooked into the tiny ring on the swivel of the Daredevle—strange enough stuff for anyone's galaxy. Fox eventually landed the trout, and referred readers requiring authentication of his story to the show's producers and "the tens of thousands who watched that Channel 8 outdoor show."

I have found these strange fishing episodes well outside the traditional fishing publications. Closer to home (my home, anyway), I came upon one in early twentieth-century naturalist Milton Skinner's charming little book *Bears in the Yellowstone* (1925). Skinner, a lifelong observer of Yellowstone wildlife back when park visitation was very low, noticed that both black and grizzly bears were often quite curious about the doings of tourists, and for obvious reasons took special interest in fishermen. Skinner was fishing the Gibbon River one evening, not paying much attention to who might be in his audience:

> I had been exasperated by my own ill luck so when I got a good rise I struck viciously as it looked like a heavy fish. Of course, since I had expected to hook a large fish, I was greatly surprised to see my hook leave the water with an insignificant little troutlet attached to it. The trout shot up over my shoulder in a beautiful arc and descended into—the wide-open mouth of an enormous black bear that had stolen silently up and was standing in the low willows twenty-five feet behind me. I felt confident that he was merely curiously watching me and what I was doing; but seeing the fish coming his way, concluded he might as well gather it in.

Smart Fish

Some of the most intriguing stories are not merely accounts of serendipitous, wildly improbable events like these. They are instead about things that fish do, or seem to do. The British fishing writer Arthur Ransome, who once wrote a telling essay contrasting "Fishing in Books and Fishing in Fact," knew the perils of sharing strange stories. But in his wonderful memoir *Rod and Line* (1929), he told one. He was playing a fifteen-pound Atlantic salmon, and when he got it close, he saw that it was accompanied by a "much larger salmon." As he watched from a distance of only a few yards, the bigger fish circled the fly line a few times, then "suddenly let himself be swept broadside on against the cast [i.e., leader] immediately above my salmon's head." Ransome "felt suddenly a new weight on my rod and could see the cast strained round the larger salmon" until "the big fish rolled off my line" and the smaller salmon was landed. Ransome had never seen the like, and could never completely decide if it was the rescue attempt it appeared to be.

Such resourceful and seemingly thoughtful behavior by fish is a minor recurring theme in outdoor writing. In February 1921, the great old outdoor magazine *Forest and Stream* published an article by a California fisherman, R.L. Montagu, on fishing grasshopper imitations. Montagu believed he'd seen trout engage in a remarkably sophisticated feeding strategy. These trout, having learned caution from "the constant pricking they get when taking grasshoppers that are on hooks," first made a false rise, just rushing at the fly but stopping short. Apparently, according to Montague, the trout were testing the fly. As Montagu put it, "if the grasshopper keeps on floating unconscious of any disturbance in its immediate vicinity the fish rises again and takes the insect." Montagu complained about these cautious fish:

> In 1917 I noticed trout which made one fake rise before taking the grasshopper, but I had never seen a fish deliberately make two fake rises before he took the fly.
>
> I cast my fly over this particular fish, and kept my eyes gluded to the fly, disregarding anything else. The fish rose twice within an inch or two of my fly, and the third time he rose, the fly vanished. I struck and eventually landed the fish. There is not much doubt but that the fish make these false rises deliberately, as a means of protection. It is ridiculous to suppose for one minute that a trout would miss a grasshopper that is floating on the surface of a slow-moving stream, when the same fish is able to take, without trouble insects which are hurried past in swift water, unless in the former case the fish acts with malice aforethought.
>
> It is a very annoying habit for the fish to get into, because one naturally strikes when one sees the surface-disturbing rise of a trout, seemingly, right on top of one's fly; but should it happen to be a fake rise, then the fish becomes frightened at seeing the fly

pulled away, and he ceases to feed and possibly communicates his fears to other fish in the vicinity, by his actions.

But my favorite story of the innate savvy of trout appeared in Charles Brooks's *The Trout and The Stream* (1974), still among the finest tactical manuals ever published for fly fishing in the northern Rocky Mountains, and especially in the Yellowstone area. Charlie told a startling tale, again about grasshopper fishing. Though he didn't name the stream, I imagine it was probably one of the small tributaries of the Firehole River in Yellowstone National Park—streams that are somewhat erratically home to big fish that come up into the cooler water when the mainstem of the Firehole gets too warm. Charlie and a friend were fishing near one of the geyser basins:

> I had just pointed out several trout of eighteen to twenty inches lying over the weed beds, and along the bank, when one of those along the bank catapulted into the air and slammed into the grass a foot or so above the river.
>
> "What the devil was he doing?" asked Pat, startled by the abrupt, ungraceful splash of the fish.
>
> "I hate to say what I'm thinking," I temporized.
>
> "It looked like he was trying to knock something off the grass into the water," said Pat.
>
> Even as he spoke, the fish vaulted into the air again, turning over in midair and slamming his tail forcefully into the grass. This time there was no doubt about it; we were watching exactly the same spot where the fish appeared and we both saw clearly what happened. Then just to make it certain, the fish did it again, and this time he knocked a hopper loose and pounced on it the instant it hit the water.

It has occurred to me to wonder: If enough of us were willing to be as candid and forthcoming as Ransome, Montagu, and Brooks, and we pooled all those stories somehow so that they could be considered as a big unified body of observation, would we reach some broader new conclusions about trout? Personally I still come close to rejecting Montagu's story outright—it requires me to buy into a more sophisticated trout intellect than I find plausible—but maybe, if it was

piled up with enough other similar stories, I'd change my mind. I just
wonder what insights we're missing just because we're too skeptical
to believe our own eyes.

Master Races

Now that I've committed myself to a Traveresque openness
about these strange moments, I might as well confess to another
hypothesis that has been lurking half-formed (and half-rejected) in
my mind for many years. It is my suspicion that trout populations
occasionally produce their equivalent of the golden child. As in any
large population of animals, there has to be a fairly wide variation
among the individuals in all the skills and traits that make up an
efficient survivor.

I suppose that this is just an extension of the behavioral peculiari-
ties that I've just noted as observed by others. Just as there is the
occasional that fish has the right combination of smarts and opportunity to develop the technique apparently used by Charlie Brooks's
hopper-swatter, I suspect that there may be a few fish in any given
population that are noticeably better at getting away. Some are stronger, some are just craftier, but I carry around several memories of
fish that stood out from all their companions in this regard.

I first encountered one when I was still new to fly fishing, about
thirty-five years ago on the Gardner River in Yellowstone. It was a
typically small Gardner rainbow, maybe nine inches long—the sort
of fish I usually could just drag right in thanks to the stumpy tippets
I used in those days. Not this fish. I hauled back confidently, and the
rod just bent more. The fish moved only a little toward me. By lucky
chance, the water was sunlit just right so I could see the fish fifteen
or twenty feet away and just a little downstream of me.

My memory of the clarity and surprise of that image has never
faded. This little fish was more or less crosswise of the current. It
had turned broadside to the current and was holding itself in a decided concave arc, cupping as much as possible of the river's flow into
its side so it felt like a fish about three times as long and four or five

times as heavy. It was as if this fish had taken courses in hydrody-
namics, if not physics. It took the maximum possible advantage of
the current's force against its curved flank. I didn't know it was even
possible for a fish to hold such a position. When I did finally land it
and saw for certain that it wasn't foul-hooked, I released it wondering where it learned that trick—and also wondering what I was supposed to do if I ever hooked a big fish who knew how to do that. As
Traver said, this kind of thing didn't come up in the books.

I made sure to file that memory carefully, more because animal
behavior interested me than because I thought it might be useful
to me as a fisherman. I didn't think much about it until about ten
years later, when I was fishing Armstrong Spring Creek with John
Merwin, then editor of *Rod and Reel* (now *Fly Rod and Reel*). John
had invited my friend Larry Aiuppy, a great photographer, and me
to fish the creek for a day, hoping for some photos for the magazine.
We were fishing the famous small flies of spring-creek lore, down to
#24s, and over the course of a long day I caught eleven rainbows up
to sixteen inches. They were all exciting on that kind of tackle, but
one was different. While the others ran around jumping and splashing like normal mortal trout, one rainbow, no larger or different-
looking, just ran and ran and ran, straight upstream. I sloshed after
him, passing John with some lame comment as I watched the entire
fly line and considerable backing come off the reel. It was, again,
like I had a really big fish on, a higher form of trout. There was no
controlling it until it was done showing off, then I reeled it in, found
it to look just like the others, and let it go. (Larry's photograph of one
of these rainbows, cradled in my hands and net with the Absaroka
Mountains in the background, made the cover of *Rod & Reel*, but I
don't remember if that was the super trout.)

It's happened a couple more times since then. There was a ten-
inch rainbow in a backcountry lake in Glacier National Park that
reminded me of small Rogue River steelhead, improbably and repeatedly peeling line off the reel with no current to trick me into misjudg-
ing its size. There was a Wyoming brown of about fourteen inches
that made all sorts of fuss, tearing up the stream in both directions

for a distractingly long time. That it was a brown suggested to me that if there really is something meaningful to these observations it isn't confined to rainbows.

I keep trying to discard the whole theory, but the evidence sticks. It's usually a fish in company with other fish that themselves seem to have plenty of energy, so my impression isn't just the result of not having caught anything for a while and being unduly excited by the novelty or surprise of the moment. In fact, that seems almost to define these experiences. I'll catch some "normal" fish and the world will seem like a reasonable place, and then there will be this strangely energized trout with a near-saltwater grade of power. And I'll think to myself, "Here's another one."

Expert Witnesses

Three years after my experiences with those fluttering trout in the spring creek, Datus and I had switched locations. He had retired and was living in his beautiful new house along the creek, and I was back in the limestoner country of Pennsylvania. He wrote this in a letter:

> This may not be news for which you have been waiting, but I have confirmed that trout in Thompson's can be heard swimming. You mentioned thinking you'd heard one and I've thought so too a couple of times, but last night there was no doubt. During the evening rise a trout of a pound or so came running down by me, frightened, in about a foot of water. The sound was easily audible, something between a flutter and a thump: not as deep as a grouse drumming. The surface was not broken; it was definitely a subsurface noise.

Vindication is sweet, even when it's slow in coming.

But historical verification is even sweeter. Recently, I read Harry Plunkett Greene's widely admired memoir of fishing his beloved Bourne, a beautiful brook-sized Hampshire trout stream in the valley of the River Test. In his book, *Where the Bright Waters Meet* (1924), I tripped over a passage I obviously missed long ago in my previous reading of the book. Greene described the difficulties of landing a fish without disturbing all the others. Being closely attuned by his profession to tones and pitches, he seems to have also noticed what Datus and I did. While he played one fish, "the other fish just tore up and down the narrow channel like racing motors. I got to know the actual musical note of the hum of their scurrying by."

I know, I know; a "hum" isn't quite a "flutter." But it's close enough, and it's a nice vote in favor of the experience that Datus and I had. Besides, Greene left much more poetic description of the noise fish make in a story he wrote for Hugh Sheringham and John Moore's entertaining anthology, *The Book of the Fly Rod* (1931). He was playing a fish when it suddenly turned and raced past him. As it did so, he recalled, he heard "the thrum of the scurry." Now there's a phrase worthy of the sound it described.

Chapter Eight

SO LONG, SUCKER

IT'S BEEN a hard fight, but now that we're living in the Enlightened Present, we've learned that it's reasonable and sometimes even fashionable to approve of animals that used to give us the willies. Spiders, bats, and snakes get nearly equal billing in wildlife magazines with cuddly bears and spectacular birds. Wolves, hated for thousands of years, now are not only okay but are downright nice.

To many of us, this all seems like a great thing. It makes us feel good to be so open-minded, and maybe it should. Of course, to the animals (if we could somehow ask and they could somehow answer), it must seem a little late in coming.

But this business of judging animals is not a simple matter of saying, "Okay, now we won't mind that the wolf eats baby moose or that spiders make our skin crawl." We can go through the intellectual exercise of changing our collective mind, and we can back up the change with new laws and new educational programs that will do much to even out public attitudes. But revulsion runs deep—our preferences and distastes, however restrained, often have evolutionary roots. Besides, human culture doesn't take change lightly, and any perspective or prejudice that took millennia to construct isn't going to be knocked down by a few magazine covers, movies, and art posters. Some of the animal world's second-class citizens are set up for a lot more disappointment.

Our language is still full of cheap shots at innocent life forms, shots that suggest how hard it will be to really change our attitudes. A man who wolfs down his food is a pig. A treacherous person is a slimy snake (real snakes aren't even slimy, so this guy must be awful). "Quit sponging off me and get a job, you leech." Clam up. Dog it. Rat on him. And I don't even want to know where the verb "goose" came from. We have entangled human traits and wild animal behavior beyond all separation, and I don't think all of them can be sorted out; the names are just too loaded now. For some animals there's probably no escape, and I suspect that the most hopeless prisoner of human language is the sucker—who, it is clear, is never going to get an even break.

The sucker is the real "boy named Sue" of the animal world. What a word to name an animal. If all the intriguing new concepts you learned about this word in junior high school aren't proof enough of how problematic it is, take a look at the nineteen suction-related columns of fine print in the Oxford English Dictionary. There you will find a thousand years of collected condescension and insult, such breathtakingly imaginative uses of the root word "suck" as would stun into silence the most foul-mouthed eighth-grader.

But we didn't stop there. Calling this pleasant little fish a sucker wasn't enough. As species were recognized, they got a second round of insults. There are many kinds of suckers, among them hog suckers, carp suckers, short-nosed suckers (getting pretty personal), yellow sucker (getting even more personal), flannel-mouth sucker (getting abstrusely personal), and chub sucker. Some of those names would have been pretty valuable in junior high school, too.

Worst of all, the name "sucker" isn't even accurate. In the modern vernacular, a lot of things suck, including vacuum cleaners, drains, babies, final exams, and many situations (as in "This job really . . ." or "This weather really . . ."). But suckers, the fish, don't. At least, they don't suck any more than other fish do.

Look a fish in the face, or, better, watch one in the water. A fish breathes by pulling water in through its mouth and, rather than swallowing it, sending it out through the gill openings on either side of its head. The water rushes over the gills, which extract oxygen from it.

Feeding is accomplished by the same procedure. Food is drawn into the mouth with water, but is captured in the mouth or throat while the water flows out through the gill openings. I've devoted the better part of a book to this topic already, *The Rise* (2006), so I'll just summarize here. Practically all the fish we deal with in our sport are, in fact, suckers. The trout that we have elevated to the most noble and rarified heights of sporting status, spends its days hovering in the current, sucking thousands of insects from the surface and thousands more from various depths in the water column. The bass, the salmon, in fact all of our popular sport fish, operate more or less in the same way. So what makes the sucker alone worthy of its name?

It has to do with what they are perceived to eat. They are among the "bottom feeders" (another socially useful pejorative): fish that seem to vacuum up the scummy sediment of the stream—fish that are designed especially to eat from below, rather than from all directions.

The white sucker, one of the most common suckers in North America (and, by the way, the majority of the world's suckers do live in North America), starts life as a regular-looking little fish. When it's a week or so old, its mouth is out on the front of its face. The eyes are directly behind the mouth. It's a very straightforward configuration of facial features, but it doesn't last.

The tiny fish, having absorbed its yolk in the first week, then feeds near the surface of the water, eating tiny free-floating organisms just as a newly hatched trout would. This lasts for about ten days. Then there's a period just about as long during which the mouth begins to droop and the eyes start to move upward; the fish shows more interest in stuff on the bottom of the pond or stream. At the same time, the little sucker (notice how hard it is to read those words without loading them, as in "Gotcha now, ya *little sucker*") changes its habits, and identifies depth and bottom cover with safety as well as with food.

By the time it's twenty-five days old, the sucker is a bottom feeder. Its mouth has moved to the underside of its "chin," and the eyes are up closer to the top of its head. It feeds by moving along the bottom, nudging and dislodging algae and insect larvae and nymphs. As it gets older, it is better and better able to sort what it takes into its mouth, ejecting the sand and assorted nonnutritive crud that got there by mistake.

This all means that suckers are frequently harder to see than sport fish that feed on the surface, even in waters where the suckers outnumber the sport fish. What people passing by most often see, if they see anything at all, is the slow flash of the sucker's side as it rounds the contours of a boulder or tips over to root in some silt. If the whole fish is visible and you can watch it work, it does look for all the world like it's vacuuming up the river bottom. Those tough, bottom-oriented lips are perfect for sorting through the plant film and muck.

But maybe the lips have had as much to do with the sucker's name as has its vacuum cleaner-like behavior. A sucker's mouth looks enough like the "suckers" on an octopus's tentacles, or like the mouth of a leech, to trick casual observers into assuming that it operates in the same way, that is, by attaching firmly to something and holding on tight. But someone could hold a sucker's mouth against your arm all day (if you were of a mind to let them) without it ever once taking hold.

There's also the problem of our irresistible tendency to anthropomorphize. A sucker looks like a person with a weak chin, a blunt oversized nose, and peculiarly upturned eyes that give it a supplicating, self-demeaning appearance. All of those are human impressions, of course, but they can be a powerful influence on our judgment.

Among ecologists, the sucker at least has been recognized for its utility in the natural system. There is little reason to believe that in most situations the sucker competes with trout or bass for food; in fact, suckers may help feed the preferred sport fish species. Suckers are said to be "primary converters;" that is, they, like aquatic insects, consume plant matter, and turn it into something other fish can eat.

Among fisheries managers, most talk of suckers is of this sort. Suckers, like an assortment of other nonsportfish, are judged for what they may do for the sport fishery. Do they compete with trout for space or spawning grounds? Do they get eaten by the trout in good enough numbers to make the trout bigger? Do they stir up the bottom in their foraging, thus releasing more nutrients into the water? Do they stir up the bottom so much that water clarity is affected, thus reducing the amount of sunlight that can reach plant life? Do they become "useless" by growing too big for the trout to eat? In short, what do they do to help the fish we *like*?

In this practical view, they at least have some importance and are recognized as real live animals living in complex relationships with other animals. Though such backhanded importance may not be a great thing if you're a trout with pretty spots and a Hollywood image, it's about the best the sucker can hope for.

But it has its drawbacks. It means the sucker is still expendable if it doesn't do quite what we want it to do for our preferred fish. John Livingston, a prominent and outspoken Canadian nature writer, talked about this problem in a book published in 1966:

> The word "conservation" means many things to many people. It is used frequently as a synonym for "wise use"—though we are not altogether sure what that means, either. The word seems to convey whatever the user wants it to. "Conservation" is commonly used by the forest industry, for example, to describe its minimal gestures toward the restoration of the resources it has so sadly mutilated— especially on the Pacific coast. It is almost as commonly used by organized fishing and shooting groups to justify such activities as the poisoning of water systems so that a pure culture of some exotic game fish may replace the diverse and wonderful natural community of fishes that developed there.

Fortunately, organized sporting groups are becoming attuned to that kind of abuse, but mostly because managers have made them realize that suckers are sometimes "useful." Suckers still too often fall into that category of admiration-exempt creatures known as "trash fish," "forage fish,"—or, in a powerful colloquialism I once heard from a Vermont fisherman, "shitfish."

It would be nice if, someday, a dad taking his son fishing would happily point out a passing sucker and say, "Look there, Buford, it's a sucker! What a grand fish, playing a critical role in the population dynamics of our bass and trout!"

It would be nice, but of course little Buford's in junior high, and he knows better. "Are you nuts, Dad? It's just a scummy old sucker. Let's kill it and chop it up for bait."

Chapter Nine

THE ADAMS HATCH

WE ALL recognize the symptoms. The subject arrives at the river, gears up, wades in, and gives every impression of checking the flies on the water. He may even grab a few for a closer look, then take out a fly box and poke through the compartments as if he's really looking for just the right imitation.

But all he's really doing is honoring a form he no longer lives by. After a few minutes, he'll do what he's been doing all season. He'll reach up to the foam patch or zinger-box hanging on his vest for the fly that in his heart of hearts he knew he'd use all along, the fly he came here to cast. He'll fall back on the most hopeful fly he has. He'll succumb to the mystery of tradition and experience that tells him what has the highest odds of working. He'll use an Adams.

These days it's most likely to be a parachute Adams, probably about a #14 or #16 but maybe smaller. Somewhere in his brain he still has the intellectual equipment to recognize the validity of traditional hatch-matching theory, and he does reserve the right to revert to that sort of thing, but it doesn't matter to him all that much anymore. He would just rather use an Adams.

And who's to say he's any less serious a fly fisher for that choice? The Adams is about as good as it gets out there. Most days he'll probably catch some fish, many even as many as if he'd messed around with all the prescribed patterns he still so dutifully carries. Besides, sticking to one fly has its own rewards. It is, in fact, a very demanding approach; your presentation and your general stream savvy have to be at their sharpest to make up for your disregard of hatch-matching's prescriptions. Sounds pretty sporting to me. But then I'm biased, because I've probably just described the very fishermen I'm turning into. Especially on the small freestone streams I seem to spend more and more of my time fishing every year, nothing feels as right as an Adams.

The novelist and sporting writer Thomas McGuane summed up the near-mystical popularity of the Adams dry fly when he wrote that it's "gray and funky and a great salesman." After more than eighty years of hard use and a series of fresh permutations, the salesmanship of this enormously popular and long-enduring American original has only improved.

In fact, the great lesson that the Adams offers to any tier who wishes to create an immortal fly pattern is its generalism; not only has it proven to be all things to all anglers, it apparently can be all things to almost all trout. Or that's what we seem to think, anyway.

A Knock-out

Though the fly is intimately associated with Michigan's famous Boardman River, its genesis involved another water, Mayfield Pond, which Michigan angler Jerry Dennis tells me is "an impoundment of Swainston Creek, a tributary of the Boardman, and about a mile up from the river." One summer day in 1922, Charles F. Adams, a Lorain, Ohio, attorney, was fishing the pond when he saw an insect that interested him, so when he returned to his hotel, he described it to local fly tier Leonard Halladay.

The enduring historic account of what happened next was left to us by Halladay in a letter written some years later to the fly-pattern historian Harold Smedley:

> The first Adams I made was handed to Mr. Adams, who was fishing a small pond in front of my house, to try on the Boardman that evening. When he came back next morning, he wanted to know what I called it. He said it was a "knock-out" and I said we would call it the Adams, since he had made the first good catch on it.

Why Adams didn't try the fly on Mayfield Pond, where he had just seen the insect itself, remains unclear, but the Boardman became the river of record for the fly's first triumph.

The one dissenting if dubious opinion I have seen on this story is from George Leonard Herter's encyclopedic and belligerently opinionated *Professional Fly Tying, Spinning and Tackle Making Manual and Manufacturer's Guide* (I'm quoting from the "revised nineteenth edition" of 1971), Herter cynically claimed that Halladay had originally called the fly the "Halladay," but renamed it for Adams because Adams "was a good customer and made the first large catch using it."

J.B. Goode, writing in *American Angler* (March-April, 1992) has made a thoughtful and entertaining case that the real insect that Halladay was imitating that day was a caddisfly, *Macronema zebratum*, informally known both as the alder fly and the zebra caddis. Goode emphasized the similarities between the natural insect and the original Halladay pattern, so we need to get to know that pattern.

The Ancestral Adams

Several accounts agree that the fly originally had a tail of two golden pheasant tippets. Perhaps for convenience sake, or maybe just because the tippets weren't all that supportive, that tail faded from the fly-pattern books pretty early and was replaced by grizzly or brown hackle fibers. The vivid Edgar Burke fly paintings in Ray Bergman's *Trout* showed that the pheasant tippets had been abandoned by some as early as 1938. Master fly tier Bill Blades was still recommending the golden pheasant tippet tail as late as the 1962 edition of his great work *Fishing Flies and Fly Tying*, though he also suggested the now-standard grizzly hackle fiber tail. If anyone still sells the fly with the golden pheasant tippet tail, I'd love to hear about it.

Setting aside this one change in the fly's construction, we come to the central question that the Adams raises in fly-pattern history: How much can we change a pattern and still call it by the name its originator gave it? By any stylistic standard, the original Adams is about as much like its modern descendant as my 1960s dormitory stereo is like the latest iPod.

I got my first look at a real Halladay Adams in the late 1970s at the American Museum of Fly Fishing, and it was a little shocking. The original fly looked—to be painfully blunt, and intending no compliment to either Halladay or me—like I had tied it. The body was thick, even lumpy. Both the tail and the hackle were significantly oversized and bushy. The wings were about three-quarters spent and also oversized, tied either upright and spent (surviving Halladay Adams originals include both upright and spent-wing examples). Goode, by the way, in his case for the Adams being inspired by the Zebra Caddis, emphasized some of these features of the original pattern—the lumpy gray body, the heavy hackle-fiber tail, and the grizzly/brown spent wings—as making a good match with the natural.

But think of the large, bulky, and somewhat rough-edged pattern I have just described, then turn to the pages of any of today's beautiful fly catalogs and look at the modern commercial Adams. You will find it in the same row with the other "classic" American dry flies, and it's a sure thing that it will look as fine and trim as all the others. What's happened to Halladay's creation?

The Style Problem

Well, several things happened. And out of respect for our sport's lovely traditions, let's start with the affirmative view, which runs like this. As trout have been exposed to more intensive fishing pressure by more anglers using better gear, it was necessary to adapt the scruffy old Adams to the demanding tastes of these more discriminating fish. The fly had to trim down and tidy up, especially when it was tied in smaller sizes to imitate really small insects.

I don't doubt that this is plausible, perhaps even true. But we should also consider the cynical view, which runs like this. Commerce deplores unnecessary production complications, and we anglers love our cookbook-precise formulas. For upwards of a century now, the prevailing "gold standard" of American dry-fly style has been the lovely, sparse lines of the Catskill dry fly. Say "dry fly" to most commercial fly tiers between 1930 and 1980 and they would mostly likely have mentally pictured a beautiful, sparely hackled Quill Gordon or Red Quill. They might then think of the Wulffs and other flies of a more unruly ilk, but at heart everybody knew what a "proper" dry fly was supposed to look like.

So it should be no surprise that in the 1920s and 1930s, when this very popular new dry fly, the Adams, drifted in from the midwestern hinterlands, it would immediately be stuffed into the traditional Catskill pigeonhole and become a sleek, beautiful, and inauthentic shadow of its original self. It is a testament to the greatness of the original pattern that even its bulemic form is still amazingly effective.

Interestingly, this devolution in the Adams' physiology took much longer during the fly's corresponding westward migration. In the early 1970s, at the dawn of the *Selective Trout* era, well-stocked western fly shops still might feature nail-kegs full of Humpies and other bulky "cowboy flies" as the staples for everyday angling. Western tiers, though beginning to respond to the stylistic and commercial imperatives of the hard-core hatch-matchers, still had deep loyalties to hearty, rough-water patterns. They recognized the big Adams as one of their own and didn't feel the need to put it on a diet.

One day in about 1973, in Pat Barnes's grand little fly shop in West Yellowstone, I was watching his spouse, Sig, tie flies. Pat had adapted an old treadle sewing machine to create a homemade rotary fly-tying vise. It was a revelation to me to watch Sig simultaneously feed three big hackles—two browns and a grizzly, as I recall—onto the rotating hook of a genuine Halladay-style Adams. Not only did this approach contradict the advice in all the fly-tying manuals I'd read—wherein it was sacrilege to wrap more than one hackle at a time—it also resulted in a tough, broad-shouldered dry fly—a long-shoreman among the ballerinas.

But in a surprisingly short time after that, the big old Adams was mostly gone from our western fly shops, homogenized away by the global standardization of fly patterns.

Identity Crisis-Free Angling

The great thing about the Adams, though, is that it can still pretty much be whatever we want it to be. Charles Adams himself thought it imitated an ant. Biologist-angler Sid Gordon, writing in 1955, spoke for generations of anglers before and since when he said that if you slanted the wings back a little you could "go any place in the country and have a common-place, staple imitation of the caddis in just this one pattern." The Adam fills in for everything. At need, I've used it as a midge, a PMD, a Hendrickson, and a dozen other things I didn't know what to call. We all recognize an Adams hatch when we see one.

And of course we didn't stop modifying it just by restyling its proportions. We've customized it in countless ways, with parachutes, egg sacs, different wings, different bodies, and different tails.

Many of these new versions of the fly, had they been originated by someone who never saw an Adams, could legitimately have been given different names. But I suppose it's part of the legacy of the Adams that we keep naming these things after it, in the hope that they will still have that magical Adams salesmanship.

Chapter Ten

CRAWDAD COUNTRY

IF YOU hike, fish, trap, watch birds, hunt, or do anything else that requires spending much time along or in the shallow edges of your local waterways, you will eventually come upon a crayfish. The first time you do, you will likely experience two realizations. The first thing you will realize is that the crayfish is already gone. By the time you notice that you have spooked a crayfish, it has made its getaway, perhaps in a little cloud of silt, perhaps under a rock, perhaps just some undifferentiated bit of river bottom where it has blended into the mud and stones around it. I have noticed that, though I occasionally see one take off, I have a lot of trouble telling where it went. Presumably the creatures who eat crayfish are better at following them than I am.

The second realization may not come for some time and may be in the form of a mental double take, as your mind fully registers what you saw and you begin to question it: Did I just see a crayfish swim away from me *backwards*? The answer is yes, you did. They swim backwards, especially when they are in a great hurry, as anyone would be whose daily rounds have suddenly been interrupted by an enormous foot.

When I first became aware of this peculiar trait, I spent a lot of time trying to figure it out. Why would any animal evolve to do such an odd and apparently inefficient thing as going as fast as it could hind-end-first through the water? Charmed as I was by the theoretical exercise of trying to solve this puzzle, I neglected to try to learn anything about the crayfish from the experts; perhaps I thought that would be mentally unsporting and I should figure it out myself.

But then one day I was talking with a fisheries biologist in the Adirondacks and I happened to ask him a question about geology. He smiled and said, "Well, since that's not my discipline and I don't know anything about it, I feel perfectly free to go ahead and theorize . . . ." We both laughed, but it later occurred to me that he had perfectly described my somewhat quixotic approach to the mystery of the retreating crayfish. So I broke down and did some homework.

By any other name

I already knew that they weren't fish. They're crustaceans, members of the order *Decapoda*, ten-legged creatures closely related to lobsters, shrimp, and crabs. Crayfish do look a lot like small lobsters, and one of their common names is freshwater lobster. Other common names include crawfish, stonecrab, mudcrab, and, probably most common and appealing of all, crawdad. There are many other local names, some applied only to a single species, of which there are more than two hundred in North America.

Most of them are typically between three and six inches long and muted in color with that intriguing mixture of shades and tones that only nature seems able to produce, whether it be on the shell of the crayfish or on the bottom of the stream into which it blends so invisibly. But they also come in a remarkable variety of blues, muddy greens, near-whites, yellows, lobster-reds, and other shades, some of which seem startlingly unlikely, if not unlucky.

I once saw many bright-orange ones in the Siuslaw River, a coastal stream in Oregon, and they seemed so vulnerable, crawling around on rocks in the shallow water, that I couldn't imagine what possible evolutionary advantage they could find in being bright orange. Gulls, herons, people, and whatever other local predators notice them must take a terrible toll. I was on the Siuslaw that day to catch some sea-run cutthroats, which I did, and they were memorable fish, but I kept getting distracted trying to take pictures of the crayfish. At the time I wondered if perhaps they had just molted, shedding some darker layer. Crayfish, like some insects, may become a paler or brighter color when they molt, before the new shell hardens and darkens. (They also are said to become less mobile and slower while all this is going on; what a great time to be orange.) But when I looked up the region's crayfish I discovered that they were almost certainly a subspecies of the Signal Crayfish, one of the most common species of crayfish in the Pacific Northwest and naturally orange.

Crayfish, being so generously supplied with limbs and other appendages, provide lure makers and fly tiers holding various theories of imitation a great field for experimentation, and the lures and flies they have inspired are legion. The resulting imitations, especially the flies, range from the fastidiously precise to the imaginatively vague. Among the creatures that we try to imitate with flies, the crayfish has a unique array of things hanging off its body for the fly tier to incorporate into a new pattern.

There is one long pair of antennae, sometimes nearly as long as the crayfish's body. These can be directed all around for feeling and balance. There is also a shorter pair of "antennules," each with two flexible tips. The crayfish's compound eyes are mounted on short stalks that give them a very wide range of vision. The "deca" in decapod refers to the crayfish's ten legs, five on each side. These are highly specialized. The first pair are the large "lobster claws," known as chelipeds, which do most of the grasping and tearing of food (and pinching of unwary fingers). The second and third pairs have small claws useful for grasping food or getting footholds, but each leg of the fourth and fifth pairs has only a single nail. The second through the fifth pairs do the walking. A fair number of the crayfish I've managed to get a good look at have been missing one or more legs, including even the big chelipeds, which break off easily if the animal is grabbed and needs to escape. A new one will regrow over the course of the next few molts. Last, they have many tiny append-ages called pleopods, or swimmerets, that grow in pairs from the underside of the crayfish's abdomen.

Some crayfish can swim forward using the swimmerets, but when speed is important crayfish launch themselves backwards with a quick downward-bending stroke of their abdomen, using that flat, fan-like tail to propel themselves along. Some species do this just to get around, whether in danger or not. It's a swimming motion not too unlike that employed by shrimp, who also bend at the middle to propel themselves through the water. Knowing that they move in a series of these motions might inform your retrieval style as you fish imitations, and though it is easy enough to imitate the series of sudden pulses of motion, it's a good bit harder to match the sudden changes of direction that might come with each change. But to fully appreciate this behavior, we need to know a little more about how crayfish live.

More helpful if sordid natural history

Crayfish are omnivores, and for all their intimidating armament (imagine how different life would be around American lakes and rivers if crayfish grew to four or five feet long), they are primarily scavengers and herbivores. Most of their time is spent clambering around in the rubble and mud at the bottom. They feed mostly at night, and some are said to even walk ashore for a look around (again, imagine if they were the size of German Shepherds and did this sort of thing).

They nest in burrows that they dig in the bottom, sometimes tun-neling a yard down. In some species, the female does all the digging, preparing the nest for the arrival of the male. Soil from the tun-nel is formed into small pellets that the crayfish carries back to the entrance, where it builds a mound, known informally as a chimney, as much as a foot high around the tunnel's entrance.

After such a labor-intense prelude, the actual mating behavior of crayfish is a literary letdown. Even the least anthropomorphic naturalist might pause to wonder how they ever got so common with such a dreary approach to reproduction. One ecologist described crayfish mating as "more or less a matter of chance. The male has no power of sex discrimination, and during the mating season he seizes and turns over every crayfish coming his way. Another male will always resist strongly, but a female will either resist or remain passive and receptive." Countless bar jokes and Gary Larseneque cartoons come to mind.

Mating season varies by species, ranging through the warmer half of the year when crayfish are most active. In some species, the male's sperm are held separate from the eggs in a cavity in the female's body for weeks or even months, then exposed to the eggs when the latter are ready. Females carrying clusters of the globular eggs on the underside of their abdomen are said to be "in berry." When the young hatch, they usually cling to the mother for a couple weeks before going out on their own, When fully grown, the males of many species tend to have larger claws and a thinner body than the females.

Does backwards matter?

Armed with all this natural history, I find the crayfish's backwards propulsion system much less mysterious. It is a member of an order of animals who, though they live with fish, have lots of legs. Think of the crustaceans you've seen: crabs scuttling sideways across rocky beaches or lobsters jostling each other in fish-market tanks. These are animals accustomed to walking in water, in any direction they choose, often without bothering to aim their faces in that direction first. (Part of the monster-movie creepiness associated with watching many-legged animals walk must derive from their moving so differently than we do.)

Having legs in water is different from having legs in the air. On land, legs can allow you to escape from an enemy; in the water, as anybody who has tried it knows, running is a lot less efficient and a lot slower than swimming. The crayfish's evolutionary track was chosen in part by the reality that whatever good its legs might do it, they wouldn't help it escape from predators at speed. In other words, there is no particular point in the crayfish turning around and running away.

Besides, it's a forager, and a tunneler, and a tearer. It has developed a terrific tool kit—antennae, claws, feet—that enable it to do those things very well. But an animal can only succeed at so many specialties at once. The crayfish is superbly equipped to climb, grab, dig, and handle all manner of things in front or beneath it, but those stiffly jointed legs don't have the power, shape, or range of motion to make good oars, especially for high-speed survival competitions.

A crayfish on its feet reminds me a little bit of a backhoe; even if, after considerable scooting back and forth, you get it situated in just the direction you want, it's still a backhoe. It's not capable of zooming off. But being a backhoe, it does have certain advantages; don't get too close in front of it. Likewise, if a crayfish can keep all its primary fighting and digging tools facing an enemy, then perhaps by backing that flattened tail and abdomen under a rock until only the big claws are exposed, it won't have to worry about fleeing. (None of this applies if the enemy is a four-pound bass that can inhale the whole crayfish with utter disregard for its survival strategies, much less its claws.)

Crayfish make their living in the quieter waters of streams and ponds, including the slowest currents at the bottom of fast rivers. They are more or less constantly in danger. Like the fish we hook that instantly head for the nearest snag or bolt-hole, crayfish have what appear to us almost a foreknowledge of where they should head if trouble appears. Like many animals, they probably never wander far from their preferred escape terrain. For the crayfish, as for a good base runner, sustained speed isn't as important as instant acceleration and a good sense of what's going on around you.

That's where the crayfish's eyes make such a difference. They're mounted on the top of the head, at the end of little stalks, and they give the crayfish a great bowl of vision above, beside, and behind. A crayfish moving backwards doesn't suffer from the same problems you or I would have if we tried to run backwards. With those top-mounted stalked eyes, it can see just fine in whichever direction it chooses to go.

In the process of sorting out the questions that the crayfish raises, I asked a friend of mine, an aquatic ecologist, what he made of the crayfish's backward swimming. He told me that I was being narrow-minded for seeing backward flight as a "problem" in the first place; the notions of backward and forward are just human constructs and are heavily loaded terms. Something that runs backwards, like in an old movie, seems silly to us on several perceptual levels. But what does it matter to the crayfish that its face is aimed in one direction and it is headed in another? It can still see where it's going.

Besides, even if it couldn't see where it's going, it can keep good track of that danger, and I don't underestimate the survival value of that. For many years I've watched elk and bison who lived with the daunting knowledge that wolves and grizzly bears were somewhere in the neighborhood. In a lot of situations the appearance of a predator doesn't instantly stampede the prey, either individuals or a whole herd. Running off in some possibly wrong or fatal direction at the first hint of trouble isn't always that good a strategy. The first priority is making sure of the predator—figuring out what and where it is, and what its intentions might be. Once all that is established, it might or might not be time to run (sometimes, depending upon the circumstances, standing your ground is the best thing to do). In any case, knowing just what the predator is doing is a really important part of evading it. Crayfish seem a little better equipped for that than we are.

Which brings me to one last and especially anthropomorphic inquiry. What must it be like? I mean, put yourself in the crayfish's position. Imagine that as you dart this way and that you are watching some immense living nightmare swirling up the silt along the river bottom as it tries to get you within the range of the "tractor beam"—the suction column its mouth generates—and literally inhale you. Imagine the rush.

Like the mayflies and other small insects who must sometimes be aware of the huge dark trout forms that loom in front of them and pull them in, the crayfish is probably blessed to lack the cognitive equipment required for the sort of terror this experience would cause us if we were in its position right then. That said, I'm just as glad to be an animal that can't flee backwards. I'd just as soon not know quite so much about what's after me.

Chapter Eleven

THE COLLATERAL CATCH

I CAUGHT a bat once. It took a #12 Irresistible late one evening on a small Wyoming trout stream. It was almost certainly the Little Brown Bat, *Myotis lucifugus*, and it grabbed my extended backcast just as it started forward. This was early in my fly-fishing, and the gnawed-down tippets I favored at the time held pretty much anything I might happen to hook, so the bat whizzed and fluttered right by my ear and out into the water. When I recovered from the surprise, I retrieved and released the bat, but for some years after that, I usually quit fishing as soon as the bats came out.

Except for me personally, there was nothing new in this experience. George Bainbridge, writing in *The Fly Fisher's Guide* (1816), said that "in fishing in the evening, it will occasionally happen that bats and swallows mistaking the artificial for the natural fly, will hook themselves, instances of both having occurred to the Author more than once."

But Bainbridge also reported on a less common catch, noting that "the celebrated Angler of the Dee, John Edwards, has assured [the author] that on one occasion whilst fishing, rather late with one of the moths, he hooked an owl, which after a long struggle he succeeded in securing!" I suspect that an owl would have tested even my hefty tippets.

Fishing or Angling?

When I started fishing as a kid, I naturally had no manners and no sense of moderation, but by the time I got to Yellowstone I'd begun to learn better. Being a life-long supporter of sporting codes and laws, it didn't even occur to me that "fishing" for things other than fish might have its enthusiasts. But before long I started to detect a less restrained perspective among my fellow fishermen.

A year or two after hooking the bat, I looked out the front window of my quarters in Yellowstone to see my neighbor, a young fire-fighter, practicing his fly casting on the lawn. A few minutes later, when I again looked out, he was crouched intensely, casting a small dry fly to a curious robin. He made some nice presentations, and gave the fly some enticing little pops, but after a moment's interest the robin spooked and flew away. Probably should have switched to a nymph.

Another young fellow I knew fished for seagulls on Yellowstone Lake. With spinning gear, he would race a bright spoon along right under the surface until a gull dove down to take it. He said that a gull, once airborne, put up a great fight, but releasing it was kind of complicated.

As the years passed, other people told me strange tales of snakes, turtles, and alligators. I heard dark rumors involving dogs. Except for the obvious and extreme cruelty that was often involved—a hook in a bird's or mammal's mouth seemed in any physological sense wildly dissimilar from a hook in a fish's mouth—I never knew quite what to make of all this. Are we fishing or are we just angling?

Gorges and Kragges

Evolving definitions of sport have distanced us from many old practices, but genuine subsistence hunters whose lives depended upon their success often couldn't afford many of the sporting niceties that are so important to us today. William Racliffe, in *Fishing from the Earliest Times* (1921), noted that ancient Roman or Greek fishermen might happily use the same baited hooks and gorges to take either fish or waterfowl, as the opportunity afforded (a practice he said was still ongoing in Holland).

Our own fishing experts a few centuries ago were just as open-minded about what they'd hook. Leonard Mascall, who wrote one of our first successful fishing manuals in 1599, also wrote *A Booke of Engines and traps to take Polcats, Buzardes, Rattes, Mice and all other kindes of Vermine and Beasts whatsoever* (1599), in which he described a device called a "kragge." It consisted of a very large gang of hooks hung from the springy branch of a tree. Baited with meat, the kragge attracted predators like wolves and foxes. The trick was to hang the hook just far enough off the ground that the animal had to jump as high as possible for it, "and when he catches the hooke in his mouth, he cannot deliver himselfe thereof, but hangs and turns about with the hooke in his mouthe."

These unorthodox but practical anglers took whatever opportunities were afforded them. Izaak Walton, writing in 1676, interrupted his discussion of how to fly fish for the small fish known as "bleak" with a note on European bird-angling:

> There is no better sport than whipping for bleaks in a boat, or on a bank, in the swift water, in a summer's evening, with a hazel top about five or six foot long, and a line twice the length of the rod. I have heard Sir Henry Wotton say, that there be many that in Italy will catch swallows so, or especially martins (this bird-angler standing on the top of a steeple to do it, and with a line twice so long as I have spoken of). And let me tell you, scholar, that both martins and bleaks be most excellent meat.

Walton apparently spoke more from his own local experience when he described a heron "that did constantly frequent one place, caught with a hook baited with a big minnow or small gudgeon." He cautioned that in heron angling, the "line and hook must be strong, and tied to some loose staff, so big as she cannot fly away with it, a line not exceeding two yards." Heron-angling had also been mentioned by Mascall, who advised you to "make your line greene, or like the water where the hauntes in a shallow place or other where he resorts," and to sink your bait at least half a foot so that smaller birds couldn't reach it.

Much of the time, though, bird-angling seemed more opportunistic. Samuel Carter, writing in *The Fisherman's Magazine and Review* in 1864, said he spotted a moorhen swimming within casting range:

> I threw my line, which was a single hair one, about a foot beyond the moorhen, and giving a sudden jerk, hooked it just under the ear, it dived, and on being brought to the surface tried flying, but the keeper who was with me managed to put my net under and landed it. It pulled about as much as a tench of a pound.

Kipling's Cow

After all our tales of angling for unexpected or even inappropriate creatures are told, there remains one great masterpiece of this genre. It was written by Rudyard Kipling, it appeared in the British *Fishing Gazette* in 1890, and it was called "On Dry-Cow Fishing as a Fine Art."

Kipling said he bought a small "minnow" lure, designed to be cast with a fly rod, but while fishing with it his back-cast hooked a nearby cow in the ear. Kipling reacted like a true angler:

> I reeled in very swiftly and cautiously, but she would not wait. She put her tail in the air and ran away. It was a purely involuntary motion on my part: I struck.

There followed a hilarious chase, in which the rest of the herd soon joined, so that Kipling found himself running through marsh and meadow surrounded by bewildered cows. Finally, not having a knife, he had to bite through the line:

Those who desire an entirely new sensation should chew with all their teeth, and against time, through a best waterproofed silk line, one end of which belongs to a mad cow dancing fairy rings in the moonlight; at the same time keeping one eye on the cow and the other on the top joint of a split-cane rod.

The last Kipling saw of the cow, she was trailing twenty feet of his line. Then "she or one of her companions must have stepped on her spare end of the line in the dark, for she bellowed wildly and ran away, followed by all the cows." Kipling's tongue-in-cheeck account concluded with a brief apologia:

But to the greater establishment of my honour and glory I submit in print this bald statement of fact, that I may not, through forgetfulness, be tempted later to tell how I hooked a bull on a Marlow Buzz, how he ran up a tree and took to water, and how I played him along the London-road for thirty miles, and gaffed him at Smithfield. Errors of this kind may creep in with the lapse of years, and it is my ambition ever to be a worthy member of that fraternity who pride themselves on never deviating by one hair's breadth from the absolute and literal truth.

Chapter Twelve

DRIFTERS

THE MORE I think of it, the more this sounds like the opening scene from a '50s drive-in horror movie. The heat of the August afternoon has finally subsided in the remote New England village. The sun has set and the moon will not rise for two hours yet, so the early night is unusually dark. Lights are winking out in homes all over town and the filling station out on the state road has just shut off its big sign. The Ferguson place, a rambling old house with a wraparound porch, sits dark and silent at the forested end of Oak Street, the porch swing creaking back and forth slowly in the warm breeze.

But out back, past Judy Ferguson's rose garden, in the dark waters of the creek, something is just waking up. Something is living in Baldwin Creek.

Just under the surface, along the most shaded side of an undercut bank, a clawed arm appears from a rock crevice. Then another, and another. Driven by unknown urges, the creature looses itself into the swiftest part of the stream's current, unable to see that others like it have crept out to do the same. At first dozens, then hundreds, then thousands appear. Something has told them: It is time. Baldwin

Creek, where little Katie Ferguson washed her trike that afternoon, is thick with sharp-clawed forms, tumbling in the confused pulse of the stream flow.

But there the screenplay stumbles. All this really does happen, but the assembled creatures are tiny, none even half an inch long. They don't crawl out and devour the Ferguson's Irish Setter (or the Fergusons). They simply drift, each one for fifty yards or so, then settle back to the stream bed. The moon comes up, the movement ceases. It resumes again for a little while just before dawn.

The "monsters" in this stalled-out cinematic scenario are the immature forms of insects—mayflies, stoneflies, caddisflies, true flies, and others. They have just participated in one of the least appreciated parts of their natural history. It is called "behavioral drift," and it occurs in most streams where they live. It wasn't even formally discovered until the past half century.

There are many kinds of "drift" in a stream. Any time you apply the observational skills associated with some of our greatest angling writers—G.E.M. Skues and Vincent Marinaro always come to mind first for me as accomplished stream naturalists—you may witness it. Put on your polaroids, put your nose right down close to the water, and look past the surface into the depths; you are likely to see some insects rolling along in the current. Some have just accidentally slipped loose from poorly chosen holds on rocks and other detritus. Others are working their way to the surface or the shore as they prepare to emerge into their short-lived adult forms. All are displaying the water's power to force its inhabitants downstream.

But behavioral drift is something more organized than the casual pushing of this or that insect a few yards downstream. Like the movements that cause the surface "hatches" that we so eagerly await with our rods, lines, and imitations, behavioral drift is the voluntary mass launching of huge numbers of these little animals into the open current. It is the displacement of a significant portion of the stream's insect population. The difference from a hatch is that they don't rise to the surface; they go a ways and then find new places to live, back on the bottom.

For many years fishermen have known that for some reason or combination of reasons trout became more active and did more feeding just at dark. Most attributed it to the trout's reduced caution in lower light; most of the sportfish we seek tend to be easier to catch at first and last light. One or two observant anglers, though, wrote that aquatic insects, the ones we generally call nymphs, seemed to be more active then too. Again, reduced light seemed the most obvious reason they moved then, but it was still unclear what was going on.

In the early 1960s, scientists in Sweden, Japan, and the United States began to document what is called the "diel periodicity" of invertebrate drift timing. Most important, they reported that the drift was much heavier at night and was clearly influenced by light intensity. Up until then it had been assumed that there were always some insects loose in the current; it now became apparent that the movements had a pattern.

Eventually, many patterns were found, with infinite local variations and "yes, but over here it happens this way . . ." qualifications. On long winter nights there might be as many as three peaks of drift, alternating with periods of little movement. In summer, when nights are shortest, there might be only one such flurry of activity. Some studies suggested that the majority of the insects involved were those closest to maturity—what might be called the grown-up immature insects. The process is generally linked to a lowering of light levels; a bright moon could retard the drift, causing the animals to settle to shelter (similar retarding effects were observed when artificial light was shone on a stream). An ecological phenomenon with a relatively brief scientific history is not usually a fully understood phenomenon, and behavioral drift continues to intrigue researchers and inspire new studies.

A case has often been made that in many situations behavioral drift is the result of population densities. When an area, whether it be a big-game range or a stream bed, reaches the limits of its ability to support the resident life forms, something has to give. Nature's reactions to a habitat that has exceeded its "carrying capacity" are many and subject to controversial interpretation, because they may include such unsettling things as widespread starvation among whatever population has found itself in this fix.

But, the reasoning goes, while an expanding deer population may have nowhere to go except into places people don't want them to go, streams provide an unusually handy alternative to overpopulation: Just let go and drift downstream to greener pastures. This, in the simplest of generalizations, helps explain behavioral drift. Under cover of darkness, which is presumably the safest time for the hordes to expose themselves to both invertebrate and vertebrate predators, the immature insects reduce the neighborhood population by simply leaving it. But now that there have been many studies in many places, it is clear that stream invertebrates drift for many reasons, including some that we still don't clearly understand.

That's what I like about nature; its infinite variety, with which I associate an infinite capacity to inspire both curiosity and wonder. Ecological process is far more complex than our most perceptive ecological theories about it. (The attentive reader will have already noticed, for example, that drifting away from your own overcrowded neighborhood is likely just to land you in someone else's overcrowded neighborhood.) As studies have continued, all sorts of subtleties and special situations have been observed. It's hard enough to sort out causes and effects in the most tightly controlled or artificially regulated situations; wild nature is neither. Communities of invertebrates are like communities of humans; though they may seem alike from a distance, each has its own quirks, limitations, and local ways of doing things.

For a further enriching of the conversation, there is also what is known as "catastrophic drift." Catastrophic drift occurs when something beyond the "normal" influences on insect movement, such as population density or intense predation, kick in. A violent high-water freshet might flush more insects into the current than would take part in a typical round of behavioral drift. Unlike behavioral drift, in which the insects intentionally launch themselves into the current, catastrophic drift is often a matter of the insects being involuntarily washed downstream (along with the smaller parts of their habitat like sand and fine gravel). Also, an abrupt blast of pollution, whether just someone washing their car in the stream or an oil truck rolling into the water and dumping its whole tank, could trigger a mass migration downstream where, with luck, the pollution will gradually thin out and survival of the insects become possible.

Behavioral drift both raises and helps answer questions for fishermen. Thinking back on the many hatches I've fished, it seems to me that on the occasions that I bothered to notice, I was vaguely aware that the insects flying over the water were, much more often than not, flying upstream. I gradually and very casually formed a suspicion that this was nature's way of correcting for the downstream drift of those same insects as they swam to the surface to emerge. This seemed to make a kind of sense; if during their emergence and mating all the motion of the insects, as nymphs and as adults, was downstream, wouldn't they progressively vacate more and more of the stream? I gather from the scientific studies and reviews of invertebrate behavior I've seen that upstream flying is not consistent behavior among all insects studied, but that in many places it does prevail, and probably just for this reason. Good habitat is not casually abandoned, so flying back upstream during mating flights would be a good way to make up for the downstream drift of emergence.

We miss so much. Most people (like the Fergusons) don't even know that their streams are inhabited by this amazing array of creatures, much less that the creatures are engaged in incredibly complex life histories that involve spending their days and nights leapfrogging up- and downstream. Imagine that you lived in a world whose atmosphere was so dense and forceful that you could be carried around by it. Our atmosphere can only do that in its most extreme and unstable moments. We can stand up straight in the face of a thirty-mile-per-hour wind, but try to stand even knee deep in a stream that is moving ten miles per hour. If you're a fish, imagine that your ancestors had lived and evolved in moving water for millions of years, becoming streamlined enough to spend most of their lives moving forward just fast enough to stay in the same place.

More to the point, imagine that you're an insect whose ancestors spent those same millions of years coming to physiological terms with moving water by flattening, widening, and otherwise developing the tools needed to move around in the aquatic landscape while keeping out of the way of the worst of the current.

But the current is more than an adversary. You don't so much fight it as cooperate with it. It gives you food, it builds you shelter, and, when for whatever unspoken reasons you are unsatisfied with how things are going, you just let go and it carries you away.

Chapter Thirteen

REPREHENSIBLE EYES

I HAD already done a fair amount of unsuccessful but sincere steel-head fishing, both on the West Coast and in Michigan, when I got my first look at Jim Pray's "Optic" flies. They were a revelation. Only with hindsight do I recognize them as a historic foreshadowing of the modern and universally popular bead-head fly, but even back then I recognized them as something very different.

Pray tied his first Optic in 1940 and developed several others in the next few years. Each one featured a surprisingly large split-brass bead right behind the hook eye and a long hair wing. The fly's proportions were quite different than those of the modern bead head. Pray used a ¼ inch bead for a #2 hook and smaller beads on smaller hooks. He painted a red or black "eye" on each side of the bead.

Though Pray's primary goal for the heavy bead eye may have been to sink the fly as quickly as possible, the painted bead was obviously a serious attempt to imitate the single strongest visual element of many small baitfish—that large, dark eye. The flies were enormous-ly popular, regarded for years as the best choice on Pray's northern California streams.

They are still great thought-provokers in our deliberations on the aesthetics and theory of fly tying. In aesthetic terms, they occupied the opposite stylistic and technical extremes from the elegant feather-wing patterns favored by many upper-crust Atlantic salmon fishermen in the early 1900s. By contrast, the Optics were a utilitarian expression of the working-class fly-fishing constituency of the West Coast's anadromous fish. As for fly theory, as coarsely tied as the Optics were they demonstrated the recognition that the eyes of prey species can be a key element in a predator's search image.

Making Eyes

Eyed flies were known among anglers in Europe and North America throughout the nineteenth century. In his milestone *Art of Fly Making* (1855), William Blacker gave us a good example of an early pike fly and described how to attach the eyes Blacker's instructions probably would have made Jim Pray feel right at home. Blacker directed readers to "fasten on the beads with fine copper wire, rolling it over the head two or three times, and also three times through the eyes, and tie down the wire tightly with the silk; roll the pig hair round the silk and then over the head and between the beads, fasten it with three knots, and lay on the varnish." Sounds more like furniture upholstering than fly tying, but similar patterns, with similar eyes, appeared in several books of the period.

Even in Blacker's time, eyes were made from glass, metal, and other materials. As the years passed, they were also painted directly onto the thread heads of finished flies—an approach that would become increasingly popular throughout the twentieth century, for a great variety of fresh- and salt-water imitations and attractors.

But we're concerned here with earlier generations of eyes, and it's worth a brief digression to recognize the dissenters in this ocular extravaganza. Almost two centuries ago, British angler George Bainbridge, in *The Fly Fisher's Guide* (1816), expressed philosophical objections to using so much metal in flies and said that "beads, which are sometimes used to represent the bright prominent eyes of the dragon fly, are reprehensible."

Most generations since Bainbridge's time have included anglers for whom such prominent eyes would have been just as troubling, even if it was only because such flies crossed some imagined thresh-hold of taste about what constituted a "real" fly. It's always been a personal call, and it's always generated strong words.

Points and Nails

But the most pervasive and possibly the most interesting attempts at imitating eyes in fly patterns have not involved beads at all. They have instead involved a remarkable feather from a remarkable bird, the Asian "Jungle Cock."

The jungle cock has, in the words of nineteenth-century American fly encyclopedist Mary Orvis Marbury, "peculiar feathers, some of them terminating in a stiff, shell-like growth, especially those about the neck and upon the head . . . . The narrow feathers on the back of the head of the jungle-cock are marked with a small eye or white spot, which appears especially taking to the fish." The jungle-cock "eye" or "nail" feather, typically the hackle point, has since been used on many fly patterns, especially American streamers and a host of gorgeously dressed Atlantic salmon patterns.

The late Joseph Bates, probably the foremost modern chronicler of salmon flies and streamers, dated the arrival of jungle cock (whose proper name, he said, was the grey jungle fowl) on the desks of Brit-ish fly tiers to the mid-1800s. In that era, when the proliferation of fly patterns was matched by a rigorous professional determination to lock in the exact definition of each pattern, the jungle cock's striking feath-ers became not only popular, but also requisite. In their beautifully produced study of the fly-tying career of the famous early-twentieth-century Maine fly tier Carrie Stevens, Graydon and Leslie Hilyard documented ninety-three different streamer and bucktail patterns originated by Stevens. Eighty-one of them had jungle-cock eyes.

Besides their apparently effectiveness, jungle-cock eyes pretty clearly had the force of fashion behind their popularity. Indeed, it's hard not to wonder how many fly tiers used them just to dress up an otherwise lacklustre pattern.

Cheeks and Circles

Other things about the feather are still puzzling. Though a great many anglers and tiers evidently assumed that jungle-cock hackle points somehow imitated eyes, proper fly-tying terminology has long referred to them as "cheeks." And when you try to envision a streamer pattern as representing a fish, it is true that the jungle cock's white spot is often more in the position of a "cheek" than of an actual eye. (Who knows what they represent on an a classic Atlantic salmon fly, which itself represents no form of life?)

Another complication is that the typical jungle-cock hackle point features a bright yellow tip as well as the "small eye or white spot" referred to by Marbury. The yellow tip is often larger, and seems at least as visible as, the white spot. There appear, in other words, to be two eyes, one yellow and one white, on each side of flies tied with the jungle-cock cheek.

Besides that, the eyes of most small fish and other prey are dark or black, while the jungle-cock eye is bright white.

All these little complications invite us into the kinds of fly-fishing conjectures that have kept us happily theorizing for centuries now. For example, maybe from a predator's point of view the important thing about the eye is not its location. Maybe the important thing is just that there be an eye in the first place to help trigger the attack. Would a trout necessarily worry about the precise placement of a prey species' eye?

And maybe the important thing about the eye itself isn't its color. Maybe the important thing is the circular outline of the eye. That black-bordered white dot certainly stands out well. So does the yellow one, for that matter. Would a trout necessarily worry if there was more than one eye?

Puzzling over eyes and circles brings me unexpectedly back to the present. Many of us have wondered what effect, aside from its weight, the bead head has on a modern nymph. On those occasions when someone has talked me into using a bead-head fly, I've just hoped that the advantage of the weight would not be completely negated by the disruption of the fly's appearance by that shiny brass ball. Maybe I've got that backwards; maybe the brass ball, a bright little circle (or eye?) at the front of the prey, actually contributes to the fly's appeal to a trout.

I think I'll just go with that optimistic hypothesis. When he developed his optics seventy years ago, Jim Pray didn't have much more than that to go on, and it worked out pretty well for him.

Part Three:
Arctic Suite

Chapter Fourteen

THE FISHING OF CARIBOU CREEK

SEVERAL LOCALS around headquarters at Denali National Park and Preserve—a ranger, a bus driver, a guy I just happened to strike up a conversation with—told me that Caribou Creek was the place to go for grayling. Some said this with the confiding, conspiratorial tone of people who like to think they're on the inside track, but none of them seemed to have fished there recently. I suspected that one or two of them never had; they were cheerful dealers in hearsay. So often, fishing tips offered with the finest air of generosity and sincerity are the most untrustworthy.

The main river was one of those uniformly gray glacial types that drain off the north side of the Alaska range. Except for the ones that host salmon runs, they seem generally thought of as the poorest fish habitat, and the ones in this neighborhood were widely described as fishless. The fine silt looked deadly to any animal as dainty as a grayling.

The milky water of these streams is deceptive, like liquid fog—opaque enough to make the bottom seem deeper than it is, and therefore oddly entertaining to wade. With the hesitating gait of

someone whose feet kept landing an inch or two sooner than expect-
ed, I crossed the few braided channels to the mouth of the creek,
which emptied into the main river from an acute upstream angle.
Just where the clear water met the silty, a tiny fish darted from my
boots, lost to sight before I could tell if it went upstream into the
creek or down into the river.

From where the creek emerged at the base of a foothill ridge to
where it joined the river, it was less than a mile long, and I could
see no place where it was more than twenty feet wide. Clear and
cold, it wound through the low tundra of the river's flat valley bottom
unnoticed by almost all the tourists who stopped to scan the country
for moose, caribou, and grizzly bears. Locals regarded it as worth
fishing, but standing there looking up its brushy course, it was easy
enough to imagine that no one did.

I've admitted before that this was a kind of stream I especially
love—origin and destiny all encompassed in one sweep of the eyes,
with all the hydrological elements and drama of the largest rivers
miniaturized and presented diorama-fashion. Each little meander
featured a perfect pool, sometimes broken by a bit of log or rock,
modestly overhung with willow and other brush, the water dark
with the promise of life and depth. Even the riffles, bordered with
overgrowth and the occasional slightly undercut bank, begged for
a few casts. The fish would be smaller than advertised, I was sure,
but they had to be there. "Perfect" was the only word I could bring
to mind, and it recurred every time I rounded another tiny bend
and pitched a small Adams up onto the slick of another pool. The
fly would land perfectly and drift back toward me over the deepest
flow line of the current—the *thalweg* of the hydrologists—until I
lifted it back and laid it out again, perfectly. I have rarely felt so
competent.

It wasn't that the creek made me a better fisherman—I don't
do anything perfectly on my own. Rather, it seemed that no other
choice was offered. The casts reached just as far as they should,
settled right where they needed to, floated as enticingly as any I had
ever seen, just because of the creek's hospitality to my particular

fishing abilities. Nature had put this one together so that I could only get it right, again and again. Nothing else was possible.

Nothing else, however, included the catching of fish. After that little one spooked from my steps at the mouth of the creek, I saw none. I didn't have time to chase the stream all the way back up to the hills, but considering the accessibility of the whole area it seemed unlikely that one reach would be more productive than another.

Out of habit, I tried to mind my lack of success and was surprised that I was unable to get very worked up about it. Though I generally stay on the aesthetic high road about these things, I've never been successful in convincing myself, as some people apparently have, that "when I go fishing it's enough just to be out there; I don't have to catch anything."

I know all about just being out there. I spend lots of time outside without fishing tackle. I also go fishing to be out there, but taking tackle along generates a different sense of direction, and a different need. When I fish, I like to catch something, and if I can't catch something, I like to know that I came close to catching something. As the bumper sticker says, "I fish, therefore they exist." Even if I land no fish, a couple assertive rises or a powerful strike at a deeply fished nymph will carry me a long way and make the day much more satisfying.

But the fishing of Caribou Creek was different. It brought failure itself to an unexpected level of perfection. So many casts without flaw over so many lovely, fishy spots were an almost exhilarating reward even without the participation of the grayling.

I didn't drift entirely off the deep end into existential abstraction. I wondered which of my time-honored excuses would best fit this failure: Was it too bright a day? Had another fishermen just worked through the same water? Did I use the wrong fly (a personal favorite among excuses)? Had a caribou proceeded me up the creek and scattered all the grayling? I was so curious about the lack of fish that I did something I would never do on busier streams in the lower forty-eight. On my way back downstream I waded right through the middle of several pools and riffles, just to see if anyone was home; nobody was, heightening the mystery.

But when I got back to the main river, I was still so taken with the perfection of the little creek and how well it fit my fishing that I kept on casting, making sublimely pointless but equally smooth casts for fifty yards down the murky river itself, my small nymph swinging easily through several riffles and eddies just like there was the faintest hope a fish would take it.

I hesitate to suggest that my happy failure at Caribou Creek was a sign that I was advancing in some way—that I was growing into some more mature and self-possessed form of angler. But I have noticed since then that the euphoria I so often feel on the stream seems to come on just a little more readily, or with less obvious reason, than it used to.

These are subtle things, not susceptible to empiricism. I'm not a different person. I imagine that I will always resent getting skunked. But lately when it happens, Caribou Creek is likely to come to mind and I have to admit that failure seems to matter less than it used to.

Chapter Fifteen

BROOKS RIVER RAINBOWS

IN MANY years of reading outdoor magazines, I had the impression that the foremost, almost historic, dream of fly fishermen in Alaska was the rainbow trout. When (at least as the folklore of the fish has it) the nineteenth century fish culturist Seth Green bestowed that magical name on this native western salmonid, he ensured that it would forever hold a place of special affection in the romantic hearts of anglers and would have an unusual appeal even to the non-angling public. The other most common trout had far less appealing names. By comparison, what literary or folkloric charm is there in a trout that is "brown," or one that is generically known for the "brook" of "lake" that it lives in? Or consider the other common western trout, the "cutthroat." The name sounds cruel and offputting rather than attractive. But the rainbow—here was a label rich in the symbolism of hope and treasure, the very name of beauty.

Anglers and naturalists of course know each of these species and all their subtle genetic variants as animals of unique and laudable qualities, but Green's gift to the rainbow was an example of marketing unmatched in the world of modern sportfishing. Add to that gift the equally seductive modifier "Alaskan" and the combination has seemed almost overwhelming to the sportsman's ear. I had caught rainbow trout in dozens of rivers, but was still susceptible to the inherent salesmanship of the perfect name this fish has. Alaskan rainbows seemed somehow like the image I had gathered of Alaskan bears: different, wilder, a finer or even higher form of the thing.

Brooks Lake is roughly rectangular, about twelve by three miles. Its long axis is oriented toward the east/northeast, and its outlet, where it forms the Brooks River, is on its northernmost corner. From our cabin in the National Park Service housing area, it was a short stroll down the shore of the lake to where the river began. We usually had to step over the lines of a few float planes tied to shore; evidently landings were easier here when Naknek Lake got rough in high winds.

I love rivers from end to end, but I am most enchanted by their genesis. Whether they emerge from a mountainside seep, gush from some valley-bottom spring, or just leak out from under a snowbank, their beginning appeals to me beyond all reason. Every time I see such a beginning, I have to stop and stare at it, and if anyone is with me, they must endure my little sermon: Right here, with no fanfare and very little notice even among my fellow anglers, something starts that will carry great changes across the landscape, that will define its ecology and may likewise shape its human society. The traditional celebration of the river as a flowing process tends to focus on its gathering of power, commerce, and history as it rolls toward its goal, and the river's poetic potential is most heavily exploited as it approaches the sea. But there seems so much more promise, so much more to celebrate, back at the headwaters, where the whole saga still lies ahead and the river's fortunes are still up for grabs.

But Brooks River is not like most of my familiar mountain streams, which do indeed begin from seeps and snowbanks and only mature and broaden with time and miles and the contribution of many other streams. Brooks is born adult, full-size the instant that the lake's surface meets a long ledge of rock and bends a couple of degrees down and over, accelerating from the imperceptible rate of flow that characterizes most lakes to the riffled surface of a running river.

Non-fishermen looking at the first straight stretch of this river as it leaves the lake and before it makes a smart right turn to begin its crossing of the isthmus would see it as little different from the lake it just left. To them it would seem just another undifferentiated flat surface of water. But to the practiced eye, it is a wonderland of distinct and describable places—quieter reaches, deep runs, graveled shallows, a hundred little nooks and corners—all signaled or at least suggested by that surface, which upon closer examination is anything but flat. Its topography, though fluid, reveals patterns: slower rippled stretches that suggest greater depth; long narrow slicks behind slightly submerged boulders; bright wide shallows where finer particles have accumulated to build up quiet shoals. Friends of mine have written entire books about the craft of "reading" a trout stream; it is a fine skill, a way to open windows on hidden treasures. Whether practiced by a fisherman with specific interests or a naturalist in a more expansive mood, such topographic interpretation suggests which types of life inhabit each place, and even from the shore I could see a number of places in this first stretch of the Brooks River that announced trout as plainly as neon signs could.

I had put on my waders and vest back at the cabin. While Marsha sought a good place to settle and paint, I waded out to the closest of these aquatic invitations, a deeper run only a few yards downstream from the "edge" of the lake. I was standing up to my thighs in the river, and the run, which was only about twenty feet from me, was considerably deeper. For the first few casts I drifted a small elk-hair caddis, a miraculously buoyant and visible fly, over the riffle because a knowledgeable local had told me to start with one just in case the rainbows were looking up right then and would feed on the surface. There was no response, so I switched to a pheasant-tail nymph, so named because its body was made almost entirely of the auburn-colored barbules of a pheasant's tail feathers, which for some reason of texture and shade and natural indistinctiveness of outline have a singular effect on the feeding urge of trout.

The response to this fly was dramatic. I cast it up to the edge of the lake, several feet upstream of the actual run, so that it would have time to sink before getting to what I imagined to be the "best" water. About the time it reached that water it was wrenched from its course with the power only a big fish could exercise. As I lifted the rod tip to tighten the line, a rainbow trout of something just over twenty inches emerged from the river in a perfect imitation of the towering leaps so popular in mid-twentieth century sporting art, which portrayed the fish as a kind of silver missile shedding water as it climbed into the sky. Before me and on down the stream to my right, this trout leaped several times, shedding artistic cliches and river water in random, sparkling mists.

One controls a large fish like this by stages, especially when playing it in fast water on a fairly light leader. At first, the fish's runs and leaps are too strong to do more than tolerate, yielding line from the reel, dropping the rod tip when the fish leaps so that the line is slack and less likely to be broken by the greater twisting quickness of the air-free fish (this is nicely called "bowing to the fish" and often the jumps happen too fast for you to do any such thing), and hoping mostly to tire it out a little. Though for many years anglers sought to get as many jumps and runs from a fish as possible—a measure of the success of the sport—the modern sensibility aims for the quickest possible landing, to leave the fish enough energy so that it is not too exhausted to recover. After a minute or two, and two or three jumps, it is possible to retrieve line against the swimming fish, getting it closer, working it toward shore. Often while these first minutes are passing it is wise to move downstream, and if the fish chooses to go there, as mine did, it is necessary to follow. I chased it in that undignified, splashy way that knee-deep, rocky-bottomed rivers require, gaining and giving back line as the fish sought various refuges along the way and then broke into the open again with a surge of flight.

I finally beached the fish on a shallow bar of small dark rocks and gravel just upstream from the river's first turn. Marsha's photographs of this first encounter with the local rainbows show me sloshing away from the camera, sometimes partly obscured by the hanging foliage along the shore; then me farther away, my rod bent in a low, flat arc with the white line stretched taut out across the current and pinpointing an invisible fish in deeper water; then me even more distant, kneeling over the fish on the gravel bar, hurriedly photographing it before holding it upright in a slow current to revive it.

If you don't fish, this whole process may seem as pointless as golf or bridge seems to me. If you do fish, you will know the exhilaration of this contact with something wild, fragile, and so barely managed even when it is in one's own hands. In a way, it's rather like baseball, with stretches of what would appear to the casual observer to be inactivity, alternated with frenetic action, further alternated with moments of reflection and even wonder. In another way, it's a variation on the photographer's triumphant "Got'im!" by which we make some small claim on an admired thing that even as we hold it stays somehow beyond our reach. I repeated parts of this exercise seven times in an hour, finally landing three of the fish. One big one made two consecutive polaris-style launches almost head-high as soon as it felt the hook, throwing the fly at the top of the second jump. Perhaps the most exciting thing for me right then was that Marsha got to see it all. I even hurried baack to her with one of the fish, so she could see it up close before I let it go.

Rainbow trout is a misnomer. There isn't actually a whole rainbow of colors on the side: like many creatures, the rainbow trout features the "countershading" so common as an aid to concealing coloration, with its underside lighter than its back. But the rainbow trout adds an almost lurid flourish: a crimson band that runs the length of its side, clear from the gill plate to the tail. This one broad band of red provides the only bright color, but it is complemented with the pale creamy shades of the belly and the darker silver-gray or blue-gray shades of the back, so that the visual effect is of a progression of shades, lighter to darker from belly to back, with red in the middle. The visual effect is also of a luminosity that in some specimens, including mine that day, seems stronger than mere reflected light could generate. It is also a life effect, for within moments after death all the shades grow dull and sad.

Because I personally find it somewhat obscure (and therefore presume you won't be interested) I am glossing over a debate among taxonomists (whose very job is sorting out the obscure) about the rainbow. It is maintained by some that there is another fish in many parts of the west that should be called not a rainbow but a redband. I suspect that this is true, but for now I side with all the casual observers, to whom all these fish are rainbows that just display different tendencies toward having or lacking the red band. Coastal fish like the ones I caught are regarded by the more critical observers as being the least colorful. None of the fish I caught had the red stripe; they sported the shades I would normally associate with freshly arrived salmon or sea-going rainbows, who enter the rivers in an almost metallic two-tone—silver on the sides and gunmetal blue-gray on the back. I wondered, briefly, if perhaps these rainbows moved down to the sea, but studies in the 1980s, in which radio transmitters were implanted in a few dozen local rainbow trout, revealed that though the fish do wander in and out of the river to Naknek and Brooks Lake, they don't seem to go any farther than that.

As for their size, I had already picked up enough local lore to know that these were not exceptional fish for the area. Wherever I go, I catch average fish at best. Biologists could save great quantities of money they spend on population surveys by having me fish their water a few days; what I land will represent the typical fish in the population, and biologists can be especially confident in announcing that the trophy fish in the population are between fifty and one hundred percent longer than the length of my biggest fish. And this was Alaska, after all. Enormous schools of thirty-inch rainbows swim through the pages of books and articles on Alaska fishing. The lodge had pictures of such monsters, many taken from boats in the lake. From my recently acquired local informants, some of whom I already trusted completely, I heard of catches of rainbows up to twenty-seven inches in the river itself. This was all interesting, but I didn't have room for a lot of disappointment in my heart right then; these fish were all I could have hoped for.

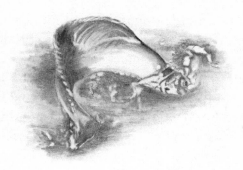

Chapter Sixteen

FAREWELL GRAYLING

THE ROBERT Campbell Bridge crosses the Yukon River on the southeast corner of downtown Whitehorse, a simple enough circumstance to observe but one whose implications are formidable, even momentous. Whitehorse, at twenty-some thousand people, contains more than two-thirds and maybe three-quarters of the entire human population of the Yukon Territory, 186,000 square miles of mostly wild, native landscape. The Yukon River originates some distance south of Whitehorse. One estimate places the Yukon's headwaters—in mountains near the Pacific Coast—only fifteen miles from saltwater, but when the river flows through Whitehorse, it still has most of two thousand miles to go before it finally reaches the sea at the western edge of Alaska.

Even if you're from a big lower-forty-eight state with lots of open country and square mileage, the scale of all this is daunting. The Yukon flows under the Robert Campbell Bridge, a nice, reasonably modern city bridge. From there it heads north and west toward the Alaska line, and then runs the immense width of that state. But from the time it leaves Whitehorse until it reaches the Bering Sea, it will only pass under two more bridges, one not far north of Whitehorse and the other far off in Alaska—the haul road to Prudhoe Bay. It will rarely even have a road along it, much less anything like Whitehorse's big stores, hotels, and fast-food places. It will be fed through all those hundreds of miles by countless big rivers and small unnamed streams, inhabited by countless anonymous fishes, living out countless unheralded lives. Here in Whitehorse, the riverbank is as citified as it's ever going to get.

And it's really quite citified. Whitehorse is a splendid, modern town, with well-maintained parks and lots of nice buildings almost up to the water. Just upstream from the bridge, the restored and historic S.S. Klondike, a grand old sternwheeler now open for tours, sits high and dry on the lawn. I'd taken the tour on a previous visit, so while Marsha got in line to hear about the hard life and seamy interpersonal relationships of early Yukon rivermen, I drove over to the Rotary Peace Park just downstream of the bridge, put my fly rod together, and waded into the river by the boat ramp.

I had been told that there were grayling right in town. This wasn't especially surprising, as I knew any number of towns close to my own home—Bozeman, Missoula, Livingston, Jackson—that had pretty good trout fishing more or less in among the stores and houses. But it was enormously exciting right then, because we were on our way home after two months in the North, and I had almost adjusted to the forlorn reality of losing access to what I considered one of the region's most delightful novelties—roadside grayling. Now suddenly a new last chance appeared. It seemed so improbable that I almost didn't bother, but Marsha insisted, bless her heart. I had an hour; why waste it? (She reinforced this logic with some endearing sentiment, such as "Don't be such a poop! Go fishing!")

I've always admired grayling. I think of them as a fish better suited to an unreachable fantasy landscape than even to the beautiful places I get to fish. That lovely, unlikely dorsal fin and that dainty elegance of form deserve some finer home, perhaps a William Morris riverscape with perfectly circular purple shade trees and palomino unicorns grazing the banks. Having grayling so handy here in the

North, rather than the way they are back home (where I can only find them at the end of a long hike to some mountain pond) was a giddy luxury. All along the highways I'd been driving for two months, I could pull over and have a shot at grayling, and each fish, no matter its size, seemed more grand a gift than the last.

But now it was over and we were heading home. I was already missing them, and suddenly here I was with an hour to kill and a river full of alleged grayling right in front of me. That it was the Yukon River itself—the river of Sergeant Preston, Jack London, Pierre Berton, and a crowd of other boyhood enchantments—made the realization almost thrilling. But somehow it also increased the odds that I wouldn't be able to buy a fish, which was probably why I needed Marsha's nudge to go fishing at all.

It was raining a little. The river was big and gray and flat and not especially promising, but there was just a krinkle of a break in the current not far out that suggested a submerged shoal. I cast a hare's ear nymph above it and let it swing around.

Grayling, like so many fish in famously distant places, are notoriously easy to catch except when they're not. The wildest, least-educated fish, farthest from the road, farthest from the fly shop, farthest from the nearest witness, can turn on you and devastate your hog-heaven expectations. If I hadn't learned that in many years in the Rockies, I certainly could have learned it again in the Yukon and Alaska that summer as I watched these legendarily naive fish follow my flies around with an exasperating reluctance to take. I watched, remembering all the while the advice of various tackle-shop experts, that "this is a good fly pattern for grayling, but it doesn't really matter, you know—they're just grayling."

So that day in the rain, when I felt the first little hit and a few casts later when I hooked the first grayling, I could hardly have been more grateful. Suddenly the whole town—even the incredibly slow traffic light at the corner of Second and Robert Service that begrudged the traffic progress in all directions—seemed a kindly, generous place. Somehow all it once it seemed that this bustling town provided just the kind of sendoff a river should have before it reverts to the immense wildness that the Yukon River was about to embark upon. And it had now provided me with just the kind of sendoff I needed, too.

I caught five of these precious fish, maybe eight to eleven inches, in about fifteen minutes. I missed a lot of other hits. Then a couple of men in a small motorboat came by and headed in toward the ramp, and the fish stopped feeding. It was enough. I went back to my car and put my light trout gear away for the rest of the trip south. As I took my turn at the glacially paced traffic light, I could hardly stand the wait to tell Marsha about the nice surprise of such willing grayling just when I thought I wouldn't see them again.

We were working our way down to Skagway that day, to catch a ferry to Juneau, but we had time to explore Whitehorse a little more. I insisted on a stop at the shiny new Yukon Beringia Interpretive Center, a terrific museum full of ancient mammal species—long-extinct creatures that had captured my imagination as much as had the grayling. The remnants of the Beringian fauna were another of the far north's unheralded wonders: Along the banks and on the long shifting bars of these subarctic rivers lay freshly exposed the cracked and stained bones of Pleistocene giants. Sergeant Preston hadn't told me the half of it.

Walking among the skeletons of huge ursids and proboscids, I almost hurried right past a small, free-standing little exhibit case that contained a flat slate-colored fossil. But something made me look, and the exhibit text explained that I was looking at a two-million year-old grayling, just discovered the year before along the Porcupine River near Old Crow, far to the north.

I think that most fishermen would agree that we come by our stories pretty easily. Most days that we're out there, something happens that, if we are called upon, we can shape into a passable narrative, a nice little tale, enjoyable to us and our companions that day, no matter how boring our friends or family might find it later. The fates are generous with these little gifts—these inconsequential yet momentous micro-dramas in which we either star or make fools of ourselves. We put ourselves out there to have things happen, and we think we know what we want to happen, but the stories that come upon us and take over the narrative are hardly predictable. Afterwards, and sometimes even while the story is working itself out, we become aware that this is the part we'll talk about next week or next year.

But once in a while the fates get really heavy-handed. They lay it on so thick it seems surreal. I don't know if this is just to remind us of how thoroughly we are not in charge of our fishing life—or if maybe it's the real definition of fisherman's luck. For whatever reason, every now and then the story gets almost too good, and if we didn't know ourselves so well we'd swear we must be lying about this one. Catching my farewell grayling right there in town, in the Yukon River for Heaven's sake, was a nice, well-rounded little episode, a perfectly tolerable and tastefully symmetrical little tale. It wrapped up a magical acquaintance with the fish of a magical summer.

But going right from the river to this museum, and encountering the grandmother of all grayling, a fish that swam these drainages before my ancestors could even *say* "dorsal fin," was a kind of emotional jackpot—a nature experience of spectacular breadth and depth, especially considering that I still hadn't left town and wasn't even out of doors. Finding that fossil fish right then was the kind of thing that only happens to writers in books I don't really believe, where the narrative seems too convenient, even contrived, like an old episode of Marlon Perkins's "Wild Kingdom," where a succession of rare nocturnal animals wander right in front of Marlon's camera in broad daylight.

Realizing this made me uneasy, because I have often thought I would like to write a little book about grayling—nothing technical or exhaustive, just a quiet celebration of a lovely creature. If I was a great believer in omens, I could read this day as all the reason I needed to go ahead and write the book—or as all the reason I needed to forget the whole idea.

But whatever I decided about that, it had happened. Even though it wasn't my biggest grayling of the summer, this gray stone profile immediately became my favorite. Fossils, which despite their

temporal distance seem to me to be more immediate than photographs and more dimensioned and persuasively accurate than
sculpture, have more of life in them as well. I couldn't get enough
of looking at this one. By the time we headed down the road to
Skagway, it was a much more memorable catch than the live,
squirmy, quick little fish I'd caught that morning.

I pictured it holding along the bank under a leaning spruce, dart-
ing up to suck a few ancestral mayflies under the surface. I imagined it dodging whatever sort of megafauna might come thundering
through the shallows of its river. And I could see it trustingly sway-
ing beneath a steep clay slope that all at once gave way and trapped
it, so flat and perfect, for its two-million-year wait for scientific
discovery. I tried to picture the vast stairstepping line of generations
between it and my little Yukon fish that day, but pretty much failed.
The gap was too big, the connections too tenuous. I finally settled
on enjoying it for its fabulous remoteness, several increments of
remove beyond the living fish I was just then regretting having to
leave behind.

And there I left it; no regrets, no hopes, no needs beyond being
allowed to enjoy it as a personification of nature's memory, a long
faint genetic trail reaching back to a species in its younger and entirely uncelebrated days—when being a fish in a river had no cultural
implications, no literary burdens, and only the most spectacularly
faint odds of ever coming to the attention of a being who would see
it as anything other than a monster or a meal or a mate.

But some stories never quite let go. Three years later, I was back
in the far north, attending a conference on the upper Yukon ecosys-
tem in Dawson City and eagerly soaking up a world of new information from historians, geologists, archaeologists, folklorists, and
native people, whose often very nonscientific view of this northern
landscape was the most persuasive and satisfying of all.

Among the speakers was John Storer, one of the region's leading
paleontologists. To my delight, we were among the people sharing a car for the ride back to the Whitehorse airport and when our
conversation about Beringian fauna turned to fish and I mentioned

the grayling at the Beringia Center, he calmly informed me that it had recently been reclassified as a whitefish. It was the mental equivalent of having your line go suddenly and unexpectedly slack. Something very big had just gotten away, and I was pretty disappointed.

But only for a moment. With no effort and to my considerable surprise, I found myself in a new and perhaps even more entertaining story. Though I've always admired them, whitefish occupy the lowest rung on the sportfishing ladder; in the traditional and somewhat narrow view of most sportsmen, whitefish are as charisma-impaired as a fish can be and still matter at all. Landing one is the trout fisherman's equivalent of what the duck hunter experiences when he mistakenly shoots a coot. Back in Wyoming and Montana, some angler or other regularly catches a whitefish and tries to convince himself (or the rest of us) that he's really caught a grayling. And now, I had outdone even those hopeful failures. Not only hadn't I caught the original grayling, I'd caught the original wrong fish. There was a kind of iconoclastic distinction in this, so I went with it. It didn't feel quite as good as having caught a grayling, but I could live with it.

Chapter Seventeen

DITHERING OVER DOGS

WHEN I walked into the little fly shop in Juneau that day in late July, I was pretty sure my fishing trip was already over. I'd spent much of the previous two months in the Yukon and Alaska, where I'd sampled what was by my standards an amazing array of fishing opportunities. The idea that here, just pausing for a couple days on our way south through the Inside Passage, I would show up at the right time for some fishing, felt like an extreme long shot. But I had to ask; who knows, maybe there was a little trout pond within reach.

So I asked the friendly guy behind the counter if there was any fishing right then, and he gave his head that slow sideways shake that, far from meaning "no" meant, "I can hardly believe the fishing here right now myself."

One of the places he sent me was Sheep Creek, a small stream that falls off the steep green slopes on the east side of the Gastineau Channel just a few miles south of town. There, he told me, right by the saltwater, I would find a hatchery that produced a strong run of chum salmon, just then in progress.

Now and then over the years I've done some pretty determined griping about our odd condescensions to and mistreatments of the non-sport fish that share our favorite waters with the fish we are so passionate about. But the Sheep Creek salmon were a reminder of a different kind of discrimination—the equally ancient and equally peculiar bigotries of taste we exercise *among* the sport fish. Chum are victims of an almost bizarre disapproval among sportsmen. They are big, strong fish. Their life histories are every bit as dramatic and heroic as the other Pacific salmon. They take flies as serendipitously and demandingly as most other fish.

And they are beautiful. Imagine for a moment that fishing had never arisen as a human pursuit. Imagine that we didn't have any interest in catching fish, much less eating them. If there were no fishermen and the only reason we went to salmon rivers was to admire beautiful creatures, the chum might well be our favorite. With their flanks jaggedly streaked in complicated non-primary colors, they are among the most strikingly patterned animals we're likely to see outside of the tropics. The subtle variations on burgundy, olive, cream, and green are enough, but they're complemented by other shades that almost defy labels. Some observers even claim to see blue. (Well, okay, maybe the off-slate-blue of certain river-bottom rocks, on an overcast day, seen through a foot of glacially tinted water.)

But all this is not enough for us. There are stories of anglers catching chums and abusing them verbally and physically, mostly for not being some other fish they would have preferred to catch—like those stunted souls who pitch whitefish up on the bank rather than return them to the water. This foolishness has to do with many things. As it happens, chums do have a lower fat content and less colorful flesh than the others, so their market value has been historically lower—though why these things should bias sportsmen, especially non-meatfishers, against them isn't clear. Chum also have a reputation for not jumping, though that hardly makes them unique among Pacific salmon. The reasons for our dislike of chum go on, each with its accompanying "but" to suggest that underneath our stated reasons we don't like chum because, well, we never did. They're chum, right? Dog salmon? Dogs?

The folklore of the name is another accumulation of imagined grievances. When I first fished on the West Coast in the 1970s, I was told that they were called dog salmon because they tasted so bad that Indians just fed them to their dogs. Whoever enlisted Native Americans in the anti-chum slander certainly didn't care what Native Americans might actually do or think, but the literature seems to suggest that historically Native Americans might feed the meat of any species of salmon to their dogs if the meat was for some reason—time of year, efficiency of preservation, and so on—sub-par. They knew their fish and made the most of each species.

Another more authoritative part of dog-salmon lore has it that the chum were called "dog salmon" because they sprout noticeably dog-like fangs during spawning. The guys standing next to you along a river are hardly the best place to acquire a comprehensive overview of a story like this, so I'm sure I've missed additional dog-salmon nomenclature lore. Whatever combination of forces gave rise to the name, it couldn't help any fish's public relations to be called a "dog." I wonder how differently this would have gone if those teeth had inspired everyone to call them shark salmon, or even wolf salmon, instead.

The name "chum" probably hasn't helped the unread angler's opinion of the fish, either. For most fishermen, the word is associated with the junk meat we toss into the water to attract fish. But according to Robert Behnke's masterful *Trout and Salmon of North America* (2002), the word "derives from the Native American Chinook language word for 'striped' or 'variegated' and is descriptive of the streaks and blotches found on the body of a chum as it nears spawning time."

If I had to guess why the chum's other common name, "Calico salmon," hasn't caught on more than it has, I'd propose that it's too pretty and descriptively appropriate to appeal to the people who already prefer to dislike the fish and need to give it a suitably insulting name. Besides, how many right-thinking, chum-stomping manly men would be caught dead fishing—anywhere near home at least, considering the exotic appeal of the calico bass—for something named "Calico?"

So often these prejudices come down to quirks of local culture and availability. Many Americans look down on the carp, whose comprehensive introduction in North America has led to many unpleasant complications in native fisheries. But some of the United Kingdom's most passionate and literate anglers enjoy the sophisticated and vastly rewarding sport of carp fishing. (The fish is not native there, either, though it has been around a lot longer than here.) These Old World experts, recognizing just how savvy and wary carp can be, reverse our own biases and refer to carp as "salmon, with brains."

On the other hand, while I and many like me look at the grayling with little short of reverence, there is a long tradition among many UK anglers—they are known as *thymallophobes*—of treating that magically beautiful fish as a pest. They hate them with an inherited bitterness the match of any of our chum loathers. We're fishermen; why should I expect more of us?

I was lugging along all this cultural baggage, and probably other complicating notions, as Marsha and I drove down to Sheep Creek that day, but in my case it was completely swamped by something else: My lifelong dream of finding myself, fly rod in hand, standing within casting distance of an immense number of really big fish.

This, too, gives me pause. Some of our most venerated angling writers have described the progression of the typical fisherman's engagement with the sport. According to their formula, which varies somewhat from writer to writer, we all start out as nearly barbaric little fish vacuums, mad to catch anything of any size by any means. We grow from that into self-competitors, seeking to best our own previous record by catching the most fish possible or the largest fish possible. And we finally arrive at a stage that is invariably portrayed as the wisest, in which we care only to catch the most difficult, challenging fish. By the time Edward Hewitt gave us his version of this prescription for an angler's life journey (in, for example, his *A Trout and Salmon Fisherman for Seventy-five Years*, published in 1948), the prescription had taken on a slightly bullying tone. Hewitt, who is now remembered as much for the confidence of his pronouncements as for his angling expertise, clearly believed that if you were serious about fishing, you must follow this course or prove yourself a boorish lesser creature.

Luckily, most of us don't buy that narrow a code. A day with bluegills has a glory of its own. There is no shame attached to it (except maybe a little if you can't catch them).

As much as I love difficult fishing for selective fish, I have never lost my affection for hog heaven. In fact, that affection has been intensified by many years of wilderness fishing for easily caught trout. The more the better. The more and bigger, the better yet. Nothing suggests the joyous complexity of sport in nature better than the bewildering process by which we define its success and failure.

Being mostly an inland and highland angler, I had few opportunities for exposure to those occasions my world-traveling friends told me about, in places where there were fabulous numbers of very large fish within easy reach. I had heard about situations like Sheep Creek, and I could imagine nothing more exciting than the chance to see if it was, indeed, possible for me to get tired of it. Apparently not.

At high tide, the tidewater stretch of Sheep Creek was barely any length at all. It poured from the mountainside almost directly into the hatchery operation, then under the road and immediately on into the saltwater. As the tide went out, the creek was left in its channel, twenty to thirty feet wide, which wound across the wet, dark rocky ground and grew longer and longer until there were a few hundred yards of it. The rocks didn't dry because it rained lightly most of the time we were there.

The tackle-shop guy said that the salmon hit only on the incoming tide and the locals all seemed to agree. As many as a dozen anglers would be scattered along the creek or bunched up near the steadily climbing "mouth" of the creek. Fish splashed and rolled almost everywhere. The carcasses scattered here and there demonstrated that these chum were typically about thirty inches long, and their substantial depth from dorsal to belly led me to believe that they probably weighed between ten and fifteen pounds. I know that's nothing unusual to many globe-trotters, but I'd never hooked even one fish so big. A bunch of gulls and ravens—and a solitary pigeon, of all things—picked at the carcasses, especially up closer to the hatchery, where the dead fish seemed thickest.

And that's another thing—the "h" word. This whole fishery was made possible by a *hatchery*, the bane of modern wild-trout enthusiasts and the curse of native aquatic ecosystems all over the world. During my long, rambling trip through the Far North, never once had I paused and said to myself, "Golly, I just hope I can find some intensely artificial fishing situation where all the fish are the result of aggressive human manipulation of the environment!" Whether fishing for roadside grayling or salmon and trout somewhere in the bush, I'd never found any Alaskan fishing as grandly circumscribed and aesthetically compromised as this. Looking up from my casting for fish whose lineage was downright agricultural, I could watch enormous cruise ships going by just a mile or so out in the channel.

I suppose I must have underestimated my flexibility, because at the time none of this was a problem for me. The raw excitement of the scene simply over-rode concerns about anything else. This was Alaska; just look at those mountains. These were incredible fish; just look at them, and look at where they've been since they left that hatchery. And this was still incredible fishing. I knew I'd think about all the navel-gazing aspects of it later, but right then was no time for ruminations. There was too much of the real thing to soak up. I could save the intellectualizing for later. Right then, coming upon this fabulous scene put me in a category of sensory overload best characterized by a comment made by a man with whom I once dug ditches, who described some similarly overwhelmed soul by saying "that old boy don't know whether to shit or go blind." Hereinafter, this will be referred to as the SOGB syndrome.

While Marsha alternated between taking pictures of all things Alaskan and dashing back to the car to read or paint as the next squall came through, I stumbled over the slick rocks down to the nearest part of the stream and started casting, but I was too over-charged to stay in one spot. Figuring there must be some reason that the other fishermen—all of whom were fly fishers, I was surprised to notice—were standing where they were, I overcame my SOGB syndrome just long enough to think for a moment. It seemed likely to me that the fish in somewhat deeper water were much more likely to have the opportunity for deliberation required to notice and take a fly, so I looked for deeper spots. I also imagined, correctly, that the people gathered at the stream mouth were casting over a larger concentration of fish that were holding in the quieter depths there. I also imagined that the fish out there might be fresher than the ones up near the road, some of whom were obviously dying, if not rotting, as they held in the riffles.

It was impossible not to hook a fish, though not necessarily the way you wanted. Snagging was unavoidable. With so many fish holding in the current together, a fly drifted through them would eventually hang up on some fish's snout, fin, or side, whether the fish wanted the fly or not. At the slightest hesitation of the line or feeling of weight, I had to set the hook, and off the salmon would go. In direct violation of received wisdom, a few of these fish did either breach or even jump completely clear of the water, but most of the struggle consisted of frantic knuckle-knocking runs. I went through most of my modest stock of freshly purchased flourescent chartreuse and pink egg-sucking leeches, the flies most highly recommended right then, intentionally snapping them off in a number of the obvi-ously snagged fish so I could get back to casting.

And here I was confronting an inflexibility of mine that didn't evaporate even in the face of such a thrilling abundance of big fish. I became nearly obsessed with fair-hooking one. I was not willing to completely abandon my sense of How This Is Supposed To Be

Done, no matter how exciting it was just to be randomly connected to one of these wonderful animals after another. I was more disappointed every time I discovered that the fly was just hung up on a salmon's dorsal or some other inappropriate part of its person. Seeing that one or two of the other fishermen had an obvious and enviable knack for fair-hooking fish after fish on their flies, I figured I owed myself no less.

Local rule and custom in the parts of Alaska I visited were fairly casual about the fair-hooking issue. Hog Heaven is often like that; when there is so much, who worries about details? It did seem that some of the other fishermen at Sheep Creek might be there just for the undeniable excitement of playing and releasing these big strong fish without any particular concern for where they might be hooked. Everybody was having a great time and it was all the same to the fish.

I finally dragged a couple strong and apparently fair-hooked fish right to the wet rocks at my feet before they broke off or got free, and then I landed one that had the fly embedded in the tip of its snout. Earlier in my trip I had been told that, according to local practice and tradition, if the fly is within a few inches of the mouth it's regarded as a fair-hooked fish, but I ended the day with the feeling that I still hadn't done this right.

As we drove back to town, I was still shaking with the excitement of having participated in such a magnificent nature spectacle, hatchery and cruise ships notwithstanding. I had a sleepless night in which vague, porcine fish shapes wallowed and slashed ceaselessly before my eyes. It was as if I was worried that something—an earthquake? The Endtimes?—would prevent me from going back and standing there at the edge of that rolling tide of fish and casting and casting until I could once again haul back on the vibrating weight of the world.

But we were back at Sheep Creek the next morning, Marsha for more dashing and reading, and me for more fish. It was still drizzling, and I immediately went down to the mouth of the creek so I could fish out toward the deeper water.

Having no success with alternatives, I put on my last pink egg-sucking leech. On the first cast, a small Dolly Varden, probably following the salmon to eat their eggs, took it. On the next cast, the fly was taken by a twenty-nine-inch chum who acted a little tired and didn't run as hard as many of the others, but whose golden sheen was beautiful when the fish was stretched out on the dark wet rocks—and who held the fly well inside its mouth.

For the really dedicated worrier, even a fair-hooked fish provides the opportunity for a little creative agonizing, because it is well known that if you cast precisely and often enough into a pod of big fish you will eventually manage to swing the fly right into a fish's mouth, effectively snagging it in the mouth. The fish's willingness to voluntarily participate in the process being an important part of the idea of sport fishing, mouth-snagging fish provides its own interesting intellectual diversions for thinking about how sport works. Ultimately it's imponderable, though. Salmon aren't the only fish that require the fly to be presented for their convenience; many choosy trout have a narrow and precise feeding lane. Intention and volition are hard to measure under those circumstances. In that last instant before the fly goes into the fish's mouth there's always room to wonder if even the most stodgy and uncooperative salmon may have welcomed it, or even lazily popped its gills a bit, just to speed the fly on toward its gullet. I find wondering about things like this a lot of fun, but I gather that most people don't.

My final fair-hooked fish of the trip, a thirty-incher, fell into that category. As I fished, I had a good look at him only fifteen or twenty feet from me. The water was murky from all the rain, so as he sank or rose in that one spot he would fade into the gray water and then materialize back into the light. I had the luxury of choosing a nearby position on the bank that would allow me to swing the fly right at him, and after a few easy sweeps of the line I did in fact feed him the fly. How he "felt" about the offering is unknowable. But I can tell you that even in the magnificent buffalo-herd/passenger pigeon biological storm of this kind of fishing, for all the excitement of just being there connecting with these powerful animals on any terms, I still found a special thrill in that first clear sight of the line running tautly down from the tip of the rod through the water to the front end of that fish.

There is a range of temperament in our approaches to fishing that is as broad and diverse as those of us who fish. I call it the Waltonian Spectrum. When we are on the water, our contemplative impulses range from the intense to the nearly absent. The reposeful anonymous anglers pictured in ruffled-sleeve elegance in eighteenth and nineteenth century engravings, sitting under a tree and fiddling with tackle or gazing serenely at the stream, occupy one idealized end of this spectrum. Vincent Marinaro lying comfortably on a lawn along the Letort in the 1940s, his nose inches from the surface as he studied the tiny insect life floating by, may seem at first glance like those quiet ancestors in the engravings, but his contemplation was much more aggressive and demanding. (It was not better; don't fall into the Hewitt Fallacy of thinking that you're entitled to imagine that certain neighborhoods on the spectrum are necessarily classier. It's a spectrum, not a ladder.)

From these fishermen studying so obviously to be quiet, we move along the spectrum, past various types of ease and athleticism, concentration and disengagement, delight and dismay, generosity and greed, altruism and competition, until finally we encounter people caught up in special SOGB moments, when so much is going on that all contemplation must be deferred.

But anywhere on the spectrum, for all but the least attuned of us, contemplation must come, even if it never develops beyond a warm memory of a given day's fishing. Judging from how often absolute strangers we meet feel compelled to tell us a fishing story as soon as they learn that we are also fishermen, contemplation in one form or another is just what we do.

I fished over those chums in 1998. It took me three years to publish a book about that summer in Alaska, and when I did I didn't even include the chums in it, partly because I was still engaged in poking at the memories. And here, fourteen years after those rainy days on Sheep Creek, all I have to show for my many hours of contemplation is this breezy little gloss on a very complicated set of memories. I find it comforting to realize that I am nowhere near done contemplating, remembering, and dithering over those dogs. As long as memory holds out, a day's fishing is never really over. What happened that day never loses its capacity to surprise and excite us again. Maybe we won't get all the way back to the SOGB syndrome just on the memories, but we'll get close enough.

Part Four:
Deeper Waters

Chapter Eighteen

SHOULD ANGLERS RE-INVENT THEMSELVES?

WE SPORTSMEN used to have things pretty good. For much of the past century we could generally count on getting our way in fish and game management decisions. After all, our taxes and license fees paid the bills. It was also generally true (though perhaps not quite so true as we like to think) that we deserved credit for ensuring the survival of many animals and habitats that would have been wiped out and wrecked long ago without us. We have the right to feel good about those achievements and to expect the respect of the public.

If you're a hunter, you know those days are over, or nearly so, in many parts of the country. It is deeply unfair, if not downright mean-spirited, that after all the things that sportsmen did to keep wildlife thriving, our contributions to conservation are now simply disregarded or, even worse, dismissed as having been done "for the wrong reasons."

Fishermen have been watching what the hunters are going through, and many of us have wondered when our turn would come. If you've been paying attention to the news lately, you know that our turn is right now.

The most superficially comforting way to view all this trouble is to consider it just a fight between the sportsmen and the anti-sportsmen—that is, between the sportsmen and the people who think that what we do is wrong or immoral. It's our activists against their activists—see you in court.

Also, when this is viewed as a simple us-versus-them fight, it's easiest to trivialize our critics. We can call them silly names, and respond to their rage and pain with taunting and condescension: Get a life, eat a burger!

The Real Challenge

We each get to decide how we're going to handle all that hostility, and the hostility we feel in return. But at this point the hard-core anti-fishing crowd aren't the people we should be worrying most about anyway. The ones we should be paying the most attention to are the large majority of people who don't have strong feelings about what we do—yet.

These people are important because they represent the real force behind the changes that outdoor sports are experiencing. Those changes—especially the alarming declines in the numbers of sportsmen and the increased skepticism with which society views us—aren't so much the result of agitation by the "anti's" as they are the side-effects of profound changes in American society.

America has experienced a remarkably broad shift toward supporting the conservation of ecosystems since the 1962 publication of Rachel Carson's *Silent Spring*. Notice that I said the conservation of *ecosystems*, rather than the conservation of some favored species of fish and wildlife or their habitats. Conservation, as a public idea and as a mission of our state and federal management agencies, has been and still is being broadly redefined. It's about whole wild communities now—the good, the bad, and the ugly—to an extent that half a century ago was only imagined by a few people, such as the visionary sportsman-conservationist Aldo Leopold.

The fly fisher's interest in wild trout has often fit well into this popular trend in conservation. For generations our literature has been eloquent about the value of protecting the whole aquatic setting rather than just the fish.

But in many other ways we sportsmen aren't even on the team any more. The sad truth is that though American conservation began in good part as a movement among forward-looking sportsmen, we are now an increasingly marginalized minority in a much larger movement. Most of us have encountered this disregard personally. In our urbanized and suburbanized society, many people already see us as (to borrow a phrase from another great American sportsman, Theodore Roosevelt) a "lunatic fringe."

Shooting Yourself in My Foot

The world of natural resource conservation is divisive and messy. Common cause is hard to maintain among groups with such diverse interests. If you've watched the efforts made by representatives of various sides to get together, you know that the relationship between the traditional fish and game conservation movement and the modern environmental movement is uncomfortable, at best. The spread of opinions and motivations among these people is vast. Sometimes we seem to loathe each other more than we despise the people and forces that are ruining the natural world we all care for. In such a heated atmosphere, outdoor journalist Rich Landers's famous statement that a "sportsman who is not an environmentalist is a fool," probably manages to offend the sportsmen, the environmentalists, *and* the fools. Instead, it should make them all think. (Personally, I'm tempted to respond to Landers's sentiment with one of my own: "an environmentalist who isn't a sportsman is really missing out.")

We sportsmen still like to imagine ourselves as cutting-edge conservationists, but the world is not impressed. Many of us still seem to regard the population bomb, climate change, and the global biodiversity crisis as issues we can take or leave—believe or ignore—with no effect on our personal futures. It's almost as if we think we're immune to the world's ills, or, even worse, as if we're simply determined to have as good a time as possible before things go completely to hell.

And it does look pretty hopeless sometimes. We are caught in the prop-wash of global crises that threaten to change our world in ways that no amount of local stream-conservation activism can resist. And like most people, we get sick of hearing about it.

But we've faced big crises before, and the American sportsmen who led us through those earlier crises were neither grouches nor doom-and-gloomers. If you look at the writings and biographies of such enormously influential sportsmen as Theodore Roosevelt, George Bird Grinnell, Aldo Leopold, Lee Wulff, and Roderick Haig-Brown, you will find that though they all made enduring contributions to conservation, they managed to do it without taking the joy out of being fishermen and hunters. Caring about the land was simply part of the definition of sport for them, part of a full outdoor life, and part of their duty as good citizens.

The many people who are working to comprehend, mitigate, moderate, or even solve the bigger problems of today are practicing conservation on a scale our sportsmen-ancestors never dreamed of. For the sake of all the things we love about the outdoors, and for the sake of the future we hope to have as sportsmen in a rapidly changing world, we should be a key part of that important work. But how do we get there?

Starting Over?

In his fascinating book *Hunting and the American Imagination* (Smithonsian Institution Press, 2001) historian Daniel Herman describes how, between about 1850 and 1900, American sportsmen reinvented themselves. The game-hog/fish-hog "culture" that prevailed in 1850, when hunters and fishermen were perceived as lazy ne'er-do-wells, faded into the background. By 1900, under the leadership of people like Roosevelt and Grinnell, and backed by hundreds of newly created sportsmen's groups, American hunters and fishermen adopted a rational, forward-looking code of behavior, and were widely respected not only as conservationists but as good citizens. Sportsmen literally made themselves over, and by doing so not only changed the public's feelings about sport, but brought the wildlife back. Maybe in order to reverse our current slide into cultural oblivion, we can find a way to do that again.

Are we willing to undergo the kind of revolution in practices and values that it would take to regain our former standing? Is it even possible? Considering how fragmented and specialized American sportsmen have become, with each group isolated in their own little subculture with their own political agenda, it would be hard to overcome our inertia. And some would say it's already too late to try. But I suspect that many people in 1850 didn't think we'd change, either.

It's not like changing our ways is a new idea. We sportsmen revise ourselves all the time. The remarkable swift rise of catch-and-release is just one example of how anglers (trout, bass, and many others) reshape their sport in response to changing times.

But it would take something considerably more ambitious than just a few fishing-regulations changes to affect our public image. And it can't be done with cosmetics. We'd have to become something new.

So the next question is this. If we are willing to change, what exactly do we hope to become, and what will we lose? In other words, how can we become more a part of the new conservation without trading away the passion and soul of what matters to us about our sport?

No one person can answer a question like that for all of us. Unanimity is neither possible nor necessary. But given sport's incredible historical flexibility, I'd say that we have a lot of options to consider. I'd also say that by changing ourselves we might inspire some of the non-sportsmen groups to do a little self-evaluation too. Let them be on the defensive for once.

But there's another question, and maybe it's the most important of all. What do we have to look forward to if we don't change? More and more of us agree that the way we're going now, we're on our way out. It's not going to happen fast. We going to fight it, and there are going to be lots of places to hunt and fish for a long time yet, though perhaps not as long as we might think. But is that really good enough? I'd rather be part of a sporting culture that is a vital, growing force for the good of society, than sit around moping over my sad place in a dying tradition.

We fly fishers are only a tiny part of the population of American sportsmen, but considering our exceptional ability to mobilize ourselves—and our strong connections to social and political power—I'd say we're well positioned to take a leadership role in such a revolutionary change in American sport. Based on our amazing capacity to adapt, and our equally amazing capacity for hard work, we could help this happen.

Hope

People engage nature, and find enrichment from it, in many different ways. In my darker moments, it is very hard to picture all of us ever getting together. Our self-inflicted stereotypes—the wine-sipping fly fishers, the gun nuts, the fern feelers, the bassin' guys and gals, the tweedy uplanders, the bird watchers, the gravity warriors, the bunny huggers, the granola crunchers, and all the rest—are so vivid sometimes that it's hard to imagine the actual people behind them ever getting together. I've personally taken enough abuse from some of my fellow "conservationists" and "environmentalists" that I'd be hard pressed to trust or respect them enough to work together. So be it—some of us may be too scarred up, too old, or just too set in our ways to work together.

But imagine if we could. Imagine the 3,000-pound gorilla we could become. Imagining that makes it worth putting up with a lot to get there.

And if you *can't* imagine it, imagine this. Imagine the people who are smugly delighted that we can't work together to protect what they would destroy.

I tend to think of Theodore Roosevelt at times like this, because I'm a scholar of his outdoor career and an admirer of his energetic, practical approach to things. I'm almost certain I know what Theodore Roosevelt would do today if he could see all of us snarling at each other over our ideological fences. He would do what he used to do. He would convene a great International Conservation Congress in Washington, D.C. He'd get all of us in one big room and give us a good lecture on the meaning of citizenship. Then he'd send us off to make a list of the things we love and the things we agree on. And he'd tell us that's where we should start.

Chapter Nineteen

APOLOGIES TO THE SALMON

I HAVE been a salmon watcher since a day, almost forty years ago now, when I stood in a coastal river in Washington, gaping at a mute, ragged, yard-long fish already rotting to death as it swayed in the current in front of me. I reached out and touched it with my fly rod, and it only drifted a foot or so farther from me in response, so unconcerned was it with my existence. I was no threat to it. The patchy fungus on its sides seemed to spread even as I stood there. Its journey over, spawning completed, the fish was done.

Like so many observers before me, I was inexpressibly grateful for the chance to be there and watch the conclusion of its aston- ishing journey. Here was a fish that traveled from the gravel of a small stream down through the big river to the ocean (for some in the upper Columbia River, it's hundreds of miles just to reach the ocean; for some in the upper Yukon, it is much longer), and then off to some feeding ground hundreds or even thousands of miles away, returning a year or several years later to spawn in the very bed from which it hatched. Only the dullest observer could miss the romance in that odyssey. I felt like I should say, "Welcome home."

For thousands of years, North Americans welcomed the salmon back to their rivers. For centuries, naturalists and fishing writers in the Old World and the New celebrated the return of the salmon. Those who have written about the five species of Pacific salmon could add a profoundly bittersweet touch to their saga: The death of every single one of those millions of marathon swimmers after spawning.

Nature appreciation, besides its emotional satisfactions, is an exercise in perspective and in learning how to stand back far enough to take a larger view. Stand back from the gravel bar and see the whole watershed, with fish moving to their respective home pools here and there in hundreds of miles of streams. Stand back farther yet and see the whole saltwater range of the fish, perhaps up to Alaska and back. It is this perspective that has most inspired writers with admiration for the fish's great migration and wonder at how it finds its way home.

But stand back even farther, far enough to see the whole Pacific basin, and an even grander perspective emerges.

Salmon are diadromous, meaning they, like numerous other fish species, move between fresh and salt water, a process that requires a great physiological change in the fish's body. So many fish do this that naturalists have long wondered what all the movement was about. Some species, like salmon, are anadromous: They go to the ocean to feed and return to fresh water to spawn. Others, like some eels, are catadromous: They spawn in the salt and go to the fresh to feed. All have had to develop sophisticated biochemical mechanisms and extraordinary homing abilities.

Some years ago, researchers writing in *Science* magazine stood back far enough to take in the whole crosshatch of migrations and come to a conclusion that, in these days when everybody is talking about the planet as one place, is especially appealing: Anadromy and catadromy show a global pattern. Fish that spawn in temperate-zone rivers move to the oceans to feed, and fish that spawn in the tropical ocean move to tropical rivers to feed. In both cases, the fish are moving from poorer to richer feeding grounds: salmon rivers contain less food than northern oceans, and tropical oceans contain less food than the soupy equatorial rivers.

Like most of our "rules" about nature, this one doesn't always hold. Some rivers host both anadromous and catadromous fish; a batch of other factors come into play in these situations, and the tangle of circumstances affecting the migrations gives rise to many intriguing questions.

But you have to be careful with these questions. You can stand back so far that the only answers are too generalized to yield much satisfaction. If you simply ask "Why do the fish go at all?" or "Why do some fish go and others don't?" you may quickly get lost in a morass of evolutionary possibilities. Faster growth (as happens in sea-feeding fish) may result in higher survival rates or greater reproductive capacity; a population of fish that is spread over many watersheds (as occurs as stray salmon drift into streams they did not descend from) will for reasons of numbers and diversity be a population better able to survive local catastrophes.

On the other hand, a tiny fish that lives in a few square yards of river bed may already have moved too far in one evolutionary direction to have success going in another. These sorts of generalizations really tell us little more than that, in any given ecological situation, nature will exercise all sorts of options at once.

Evolutionary directions taken by species aren't the result of conscious decisions. No one ever promised salmon that in the long run becoming anadromous would be just the thing. They evolved in that direction for no more reason than that their habitat, physiology, and appetite permitted them to. We can assume they're still evolving. Indeed, there are a number of fish species in North America that live primarily in rivers but occasionally run down to the tidewater for a few meals, kind of doodling around in the brine for a while like they're waiting for the next excursion boat to Vancouver. (One imagines a pair of them, a male and female in a Gary Larsonesque cartoon, standing around discussing it. She says, "All the neighbors are becoming anadromous, but do you ever take me to Alaska? Noooo.")

So perhaps the question is: Where is all this traveling getting the salmon, besides right back where they started? Are they going somewhere in particular, evolutionarily? Or, to ask the question from the bottom-line perspective: Was anadromy a good idea?

Anybody who has followed modern fisheries management knows that anadromy's gotten them into a lot of trouble with humans. Periodically gathering your whole population up and cramming it into small exposed spaces is only a good way to make it as a wild animal if you're prepared to take some pretty heavy losses from predators. Pacific salmon thrived for millennia despite many predators, including native Americans. But European technology and greed were too much for them. Long before we developed ways to decimate oceanic fish populations, we were hauling salmon out of streams in disastrous numbers.

So the answer may be, yes, anadromy works pretty well, as long as you don't encounter some fabulously overevolved predator, that once-in-a-billion-year freak (let's face it, we're not your normal animal) that is the average species' equivalent of an Act of God.

Salmon have made a magnificent adjustment to the food-poor rivers where they spawn; when they return from the ocean, they eat virtually nothing while in fresh water. (This is also true of Atlantic salmon and steelhead trout, two species that live to spawn repeatedly.) This grand mass of animal life sweeps into the rivers with a single appetite, one that makes no nutrient demands on the river's biological resources, but contributes to them enormously.

When tons of fish come up from the sea, many a wild creature gets fed, from micro-organisms to mink to bears to eagles. Some feed in the water, some haul salmon a hundred yards from the stream to be eaten at their leisure. Many eat what's left after someone else has had the first course.

I first learned about this scattering of organic bounty more than twenty years ago, when a biologist friend of mine, Doug Houston, sent me a study he'd been involved in. Conducted by the Washington Department of Natural Resources and the National Park Service on the Olympic Peninsula, the paper had the happy title of "Ecology of

Dead Salmon." The researchers tagged nearly a thousand carcasses and installed tiny radio transmitters in 174 more, on four streams, in order to track just what became of all that fish meat. They described the fate of a typical coho salmon carcass:

> A sequence commonly observed was for raccoons, otters, or bears to retrieve carcasses from the stream (bears removed fish from pools more than 1.5 meters deep), to feed, and then to move on. The scattered remains were next consumed over several weeks by small mammals and birds, until only scattered bones and pyloric caeca remained.

These leftovers, the report went on, frequently showed the tiny toothmarks of shrews and rodents, suggesting that eventually every piece of salmon would be consumed, digested, and then distributed on the forest floor. To all of those salmon eaters, yes, anadromy was a good idea.

There have now been a number of these studies, and they tell an elegantly complex story of nature at its most self-nurturing. A lot of salmon meat isn't consumed by birds and land mammals. If the river is too deep or too swift, or for some other reason has stretches inaccessible to predators and scavengers, the dead fish remain in the stream, where they decay and may have a substantial effect on the basic organic character of the stream. As gardeners know, fish make great fertilizer; imagine what a few thousand twenty-five-pound salmon would do for the aquatic vegetative growth in a mile of river. In the organic fortunes of the river, anadromy must be judged a terrific idea. It's why some people now talk about figuring how to replace the nutrients we've taken when we removed all those salmon.

With this information in mind, you don't have to stand back farther and farther to know what's going on. You can stand right up close to the river and see what an awful tragedy it is that the great salmon runs that once filled it are mostly gone. It's not just the loss of a beautiful animal migration spectacle or of good fishing. The spawning run isn't an event; it's a process. When those millions of carcasses are no longer feeding all the creatures that lived along the stream, the scavenger and predator populations decline or disappear. When carcasses no longer settle to the bottom or get hung up in streambed tangles, the stream's nutrient load declines, and its capacity for supporting other life forms does too.

To make matters worse, humanity's ambitious labors at "improvement" of navigational channels—and beautifying rivers in general—have resulted in the removal of all the stumps, snags, beaver workings, and other obstructions that for thousands of years not only provided shelter for living fish but also held carcasses in place after the fish died. Thanks to our misguided good intentions, many rivers that were once heavily laced with natural nutrient traps now give water a straight shot to the sea, and flush out clean in a good freshet.

So I finally stand back far enough to come full circle and, like the salmon, return to the shallow gravel bar where we started, one haggard, frayed old hen salmon and one puzzled, awed fisherman. The odds against her getting home were great enough before we started messing around with her river; now it seems amazing that any of her kind show up at all and sad that she won't even be able to die and rot the way she once would have. My sadness isn't the result of some anthropomorphic concern that she be allowed to die a dignified, natural death. I couldn't begin to define such a thing. My sadness is that she represents something badly and ignorantly damaged.

Still, for all my resistance to anthropomorphism, it seems to me that as I watch her swim listlessly up the gravel bar to a quiet resting place, an apology might be more in order than a welcome.

Chapter Twenty

CRAZY COOTS AND MERE FARRAGOS

IN THE past couple years I've enjoyed reading several articles that summarize this or that list of the best fishing books—the best stories, the best entomological treatises, that sort of thing. This is a long-honored tradition in fly-fishing writing; we've always been fond of praising not only our betters but our pals, and that's one of the many civil things about the sport that attracts me.

But even a good thing can be carried too far. We need to keep our balance amidst all the self-congratulatory preening about our great writers. In fact, we need reminding of how genuinely wretched angling writing can get when it is undertaken by someone with special gifts for the work.

Here in the Western Hemisphere, mention of lists of great fishing writers inevitably leads to thoughts of the late Arnold Gingrich, American fly fishing's congenial toastmaster of the 1970s. Gingrich (I never met him, but so collegial are his books that I always think of him as "Arnold") specialized in such lists, culled from his voluminous reading. For a while there, Arnold was American fly fishing's foremost guide through the sport's literary labyrinths, even if most

of us couldn't afford to buy—or even travel far enough to see—
copies of a lot of the books he mentioned.

I came to fly fishing during Arnold's reign as the sport's principal
commentator, and it took me a long time to catch on to the darker
side of what he accomplished. Being fundamentally well mannered,
he avoided offering much in the way of criticism. This might seem
to have been an odd position for the founding editor of *Esquire*,
for many years one of America's most literate and discriminating
magazines. But I suspect that one of the reasons that Arnold enjoyed
being part of fly fishing's little world was because it was so unde-
manding that way. He could take it easy and just have fun. Besides,
being who he was in the big world of American letters, any judgment
he did choose to offer on fly-fishing writing instantly went right to
the top among the opinion makers, so there was no pressure on him
to compete for an audience. Why be unpleasant?

Anyway, in his lists and other commentary, though he occasionally said sharply critical things about someone, Arnold mostly told the
happy story of the great books, the ones we could generally agree on
as essential if not immortal. This worked well for most of his readers, but it also meant that he either left out or said too little about
some of the most interesting stuff, which has of course been some
of the worst stuff.

Noticing all this, I have wondered if we need a list of Fly Fishing's
Greatest Dogs—the "classic" (to employ angling writing's most
over-used literary adjective) worst books. After all, most people
enjoy watching other people's failures. The "Darwin Awards," given
annually to people so erring in their ways that they eliminate themselves from the gene pool, are big news. People conduct that same
sort of negative-celebration exercise with cars (Edsel fans aside),
fashion (when I look at the pictures of this year's "best-dressed"
and "worst-dressed," I can't tell them apart) and all manner of other
categories of endeavor. It seemed obvious to me that we need a list
of these awful books.

But after putting a little time into this, I find it a surprisingly tricky
list to compile. Everyone knows that there have been countless

undistinguished fishing books, all perfectly forgettable. But that doesn't make them bad, does it? After all, they did their job. They provided anglers with lots of useful information, and then they became out of date, or were replaced by better books, or just faded away. Fishing books, like mysteries, economics tracts, travel books, cookbooks, and campaign biographies, naturally tend to have a short life expectancy. Failing to earn their authors immortality is hardly a useful measure of their practical worth. Only one of us gets to be Walton.

No, if you want to write an authentically terrible fishing book, mediocrity isn't good enough. You have to stand out somehow. You have to really stink, and the aroma must remain potent across many generations.

Still, it's a tough list to compile even on those terms.

I started poorly, assuming this was a subject on which I could easily get advice. I asked some very well-read friends to name a few older angling books that they thought measured up to this high standard and that might be considered genuinely deathless junk. Their response was kind of helpful, but it was also a shock, because they despised a couple books that I always thought were pretty swell. Rather than try to figure out which of us was the Edsel fan, I backed off and decided to go it on my own, following the trail of some earlier critics who have singled out this or that book for its special awfulness.

The earliest book to get this kind of attention may have been Richard Franck's *Northern Memoirs*, written in 1658 but not published until 1694. (The delay should be a clue, I suppose; did the rejection letters just take a really long time to get delivered back then?) As angling historian John Waller Hills, writing in *A History of Fly Fishing for Trout* (1921), put it, Franck was a terrible writer,

> "possessor of the most turgid and pedantic style with which mortal was ever afflicted. . . . The style of the book may be judged from its title: *Northern Memoirs, Calculated for the Meridian of Scotland. Wherein most or all of the Cities, Citadels, Seaports, Castles, Forts, Fortresses, Rivers and Rivulets are compendiously*

described. Together with choice Collections of Various Discoveries,
Remarkable Observations, Theological Notions, Potilical Axioms,
National Intrigues . . . ."

Well, the title goes on like that for a long time. After a while, it even
mentions fishing.

And, not content with his vile writing style, Franck took time to
villify Izaak Walton himself, further alienating many readers. Even
the congenial Gingrich (a devout Walton reader), called Franck a
"crazy coot."

On the other hand, Franck contributed some of our earliest
expert writing on Atlantic salmon fishing. N.W. Simmonds, in *Ear-*
ly Scottish Angling Literature (1997), captured the ambivalence we
must feel about Franck, when he wrote that "he was a Cromwellian
trooper, a religious bigot, a bag of wind and an abominable writer
but he was clearly a real angler who fished in Scotland and possessed much knowledge." Readers willing to plow through his
prose could learn a lot. This sort of authoritative usefulness kind
of compromises the classic awfulness of Franck's book. Let's try
another.

And let's skip the 1700s—hastily passing over some writers
whose only distinction was that they had the good taste to know
who to plagiarize—to a singularly annoying little book by another
British writer, Robert Blakey's *Historical Sketches of Angling Lit-*
erature of All Nations (1856). This book was so full of mystifying
information and apparent lies that Thomas Westwood and Thomas Satchell, in *Bibliotheca Piscatoria* (1883), delivered against
it my all-time favorite literary bash: "A slip-shod and negligent
work, devoid of all real utility. A mere farrago of matter relevant
and irrelevant, of indiscriminate sweepings from miscellaneous
sources, of quotations incorrectly given and of so-called original
passages the vagueness and uncertainty of which rob them of all
weight and value."

And yet for his day, Blakey wasn't all that bad a writer. As long
ago as 1894, *Fishing Gazette* editor R.B. Marston, while admitting

that Blakey "made some very curious blunders in dates, etc.," said that he deserved our "critical indulgence." Besides, Blakey produced several other works on angling that were very well thought of. Vexing man, but I'm not sure his book measures up to our criteria. Hardly any modern fly-fishing readers have ever even heard of it and that doesn't indicate the Edsel-grade level of immortality we're looking for here.

Some have singled out W.C. Prime's *I Go A-Fishing* (1873) as a true Turd in the Literary Punchbowl. It was Gingrich who noted that the title itself is something of an error, and indeed, the book could have had a subtitle, *But don't expect to read about it here*. As Gingrich said in *The Joys of Trout* (1973), "trying to get to the fishing in Prime is like the proverbial attempt to pick flyspecks out of pepper with boxing gloves on."

So I'm not sure if this makes it a bad fishing book or just makes it not a fishing book at all. It's easy and enjoyable enough to read, if you don't care that you're not reading about a guy who actually did go a-fishing.

George Kelson's magnificently produced and encyclopedic *The Salmon Fly* (1895) has gotten its share of votes, too. Kelson was among the rulers of the British salmon scene for many years, and his big book has experienced occasional reprinting to satisfy the recent need for authoritative information on those grand old patterns. But as Andrew Herd explained in *The Fly* (2001), Kelson eventually got thoroughly and deservedly crosswise of his fellow anglers, and in a devastating published debate with the same R.B. Marston mentioned above for his kindly defense of Blakey, "Kelson's credibility was shattered." His general arrogance (Herd refers to Kelson's "breathtaking chutzpah"), his goofy natural history, his passionate devotion to absurdly obscure details, and his willingness to take credit for patterns apparently developed by others, eventually did him in.

But people still cherish his book. I'd love to own a copy myself. Atlantic salmon fly tiers with an interest in the traditional Victorian-era patterns admire it with near-scriptural intensity, even if they ignore Kelson's ditherings. If a fishing book has this long and hearty a life, even if it does so despite the author's arrogance, can it really be all that bad?

Louis Rhead's *American Trout Stream Insects* (1916) occupies the most peculiar position of all in angling entomology. Rather than being judged merely bad, it has become thought of as the great literary tragedy of that field. Rhead, a gifted, widely honored commerical artist and illustrator who wrote or edited several other excellent fishing books, studied the stream insects and forage fish in eastern American streams (well, those near New York, anyway) for several seasons. His book contained lively and convincing color portraits of them, as well as his idiosyncratic fly patterns. But he ignored scientific nomenclature in his hatch catalog and completely abandoned several centuries-worth of existing fly patterns. By thus cutting himself off from the known traditions and wisdoms, he committed both literary and commercial suicide. As Gingrich put it, "Rhead's remarkably original work, perceptive almost to the point of divination and augury, was too generally shrugged off as the amateurish fancy of a dilettante, or dismissed as a sales gimmick for specific flies of his own creation. . . ." (There was more to Rhead's failure, by the way. The New York angling establishment of his day apparently had it in for him, and it isn't fully clear why. But it cost him.)

So is this book of Rhead's authentically bad, or just misguided, or the victim of circumstances? His failure was so spectacular that it alone has guaranteed a sort of perverse immortality for him, as an object lesson for later writers. But is that enough to make our short list of Fly Fishing Flops? I'm not sure. Gingrich was right; there was something very like genius at work in Rhead's book and if it went wrong it still had things to teach us. It was, as the saying goes, a glorious failure. And his illustrations of angling scenes made him the Dave Whitlock of his time. Rhead's distinctive pen-and-ink portrayals of fly fishers on the stream are still among my favorites; I am very pleased to have one on the cover of my history of American Fly Fishing.

(Rhead's career ended in a fittingly quirky way. According to the obituary in *The New York Times*, July 30, 1926, Rhead died from heart failure some days after a Herculean struggle landing a thirty-pound turtle with hook and line. The turtle had been "devastating trout ponds on his place.")

One last problematic expert demands our attention. I conclude my list with a bow toward my personal favorite "bad" book, Minnesota tackle merchandiser George Leonard Herter's nearly monumental, *Professional Fly Tying, Spinning and Tackle Making Manual and Manufacturer's Guide*, first published in 1941. My copy is the "revised nineteenth edition," published in 1971. At 584 pages of small print, it is one of the longest and most information-packed fishing books by any single author, ever. And I include it here for one reason only: His conspicuous absence from conversations on the subject of angling literature in the sport's more urbane and proper circles. Except for Montana writer Charles Brooks, who mentioned Herter's book fondly a couple of times in his own books, who would never have characterized himself as urbane *or* proper, and who, I think, sensed a kindred spirit in Herter's brusque pronouncements, the literary authorities in angling-writing's mainstream seem usually to have pretended that this very briskly selling book didn't exist. Herter or his book apparently somehow so offended Gingrich and the other modern tastemakers that they effectively eliminated him from their consciousness, and, thus, from the consciousnesses of their readers.

Herter was certainly an outsider, a boisterously self-promotional, unpolished, and belligerently confident writer from America's uncosmopolitan upper Midwest. He was socially remote from the refined sensitivities of the East-Coast centers of angling leadership. He also was inclined to take broad credit for a lot of stuff and to verbally dump all over competing credit-takers whom had long been sainted by the angling establishment. None of this would have helped endear him to the sport's literary chroniclers.

Whatever Herter's offense may have been, it resulted in a strange professional isolation that seems more mystifying to me as the years pass. It is mystifying because someone, in fact quite a lot of someones, still managed to find and buy the book. In 1953, for example, Herter claimed that 400,000 copies had already been sold, a fabulously successful sales for any book in any category, much less for a book in a field where the sale of 20,000 copies is a pretty big deal even today.

Do I believe Herter that it really sold that many copies? Maybe, maybe not. Having a widely distributed (and equally outspoken) catalog in which to steadily promote a book makes a huge difference for sales, no question about that. I do know that the book had more reprintings than almost all other modern fishing books, and even if the printings were small, it must have sold a lot of copies.

So for all his irritating, opinionated, and sometimes off-track pronouncements, Herter seemed to have a huge reach among anglers, at least before the fly-fishing renaissance that began in the 1970s (the 1974 Herter's catalog included testimonials for the book by Herbert Hoover, Ted Trueblood, and others). His book, like his opinions, was fairly homemade (as were his other books, such singular titles as the *Bull Cook Book*, in three volumes, and his manual on life, written with his wife Berthe, *How to Live with a Bitch*). He displayed the worst traits of many of his predecessors in this little Junk-Book Sweepstakes I'm running here. He was Franckian in his self-importance. He was Kelsonian in that he claimed to have originated a lot of things that the mainstream writers saw as having other originators. He was Rheadian in his creation of his own name-brand flies, perhaps most notably showcased in his series of laughably unrealistic color drawings of his own streamer patterns.

On the other hand, he was, at least by his own account, vastly experienced in fly fishing, and he mixed relentless crankiness with a startling awareness of environmental issues. And his book is undeniably full of really useful information and advice. Maybe that mixture of combativeness, sensitivity, expertise, and weirdness was just too much for our more genteel writers to deal with. But they should have tried.

Enough. Others come to mind and demand their turn. I could exercise my moods on Frank Forester or Charles Southard or several others, but I think a pattern has already emerged. This isn't working very well. Despite the occasional literary outrage in our history, it's hard to make a good list of bad books (and, yes, I've chickened out entirely when it comes to dealing with the books of living writers). We each may recall a few books that we disliked, but as a group we fly fishers just haven't been directed toward systematic disapproval the way some other passionate specialists seem to be. Even the few books that past generations have gone out of their way to revile haven't been without merit and friends.

We seem to cherish our cranks and our crackpots almost as much as we adore our geniuses, and on our more lucid days we have to admit that the line between these types is probably pretty thin.

As a writer and as a believer in the free speech that is the only hope for writers and readers anyway, I have trouble with the very concept of a "bad book." There are books by stupid authors, misguided authors, painfully untalented authors, dishonest authors, brilliant but twisted authors, pedestrian authors, and authors who are genuinely bad people. But none of that is ever the book's fault, is it?

It may not be true that I never met a fishing book I didn't like, but I've only met a few that were irritating enough to get seriously worked up about. As much time as we fly fishers have spent disagreeing about this or that theory or technique, most of us do seem to have maintained a healthy tolerance for our writers. They're probably about as good as we deserve, and there seems little question that they're as good as we want them to be.

Besides, judging from the number of passionate and erudite bibliographers that fly-fishing has inspired just in the past two centuries, I am inclined to accept the wisdom of the ever-erudite G.E.M. Skues, who said that "in angling literature it is a matter of observation that no book, however worthless, from the point of view of literature or teaching, ever dies."

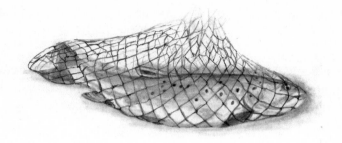

Chapter Twenty-one

HOW CAN YOU DO THAT?

I RECENTLY attended a conference on the importance of protecting wild places. There was a roundtable discussion in which about twenty devoted conservationists were comparing notes on things that they found especially powerful in their own experiences of nature. After several others had spoken, including a hunter or two, I mentioned something about the connection to be had with the natural world in the instant of the fish's strike—what the great writer Isak Dinesen, after shooting a lion, described like this:

> I stood, panting, in the grass, aglow with the plentipotence that a shot gives you, because you take effect at a distance.

I used the example of that "taking effect"—when I felt the first strike and pull of a fish—as one of those powerful moments in our contact with nature. I think this was okay with the people at the conference. But then I happened to mention releasing the fish and instantly some of the other conferees were on the attack. One referred to what I was doing as "Catch-and-Maim." They kept asking, in various ways, "How can you *do* that?" Their self-righteousness so overwhelmed my own that I not only shut up, but I also fled from the conference soon after. I was caught so off guard that I simply had no idea what else I might say that would provoke another ambush. I had mistakenly assumed we were all on the some similar "side" in the struggle to save wildness.

It wasn't that I hadn't heard it all before. I'm sure I could have stated their arguments as well as they did, having studied the evolution of attitudes toward wildlife more than they had, and having also had abundant time, while catching and releasing thousands of fish—looking again and again into those myopic unblinking baffled eyes—to reflect on the moral and emotional implications of what I was doing. I knew what they were talking about. What was so hard to take was the absolute intractability of their attack.

Since its appearance as a management approach more than fifty years ago, catch-and-release fishing has been heralded as the salvation of countless fisheries. As fishery resources were threatened with overuse and collapse of fish populations, it seemed to forward-looking managers and anglers that they might at least save one exciting part of the experience—the thrill of catching the fish in the first place. Given the right kinds of tackle (no organic bait, which fish tend to swallow deeply), only a tiny percentage of the released fish die. Catch-and-release regulations worked, and proved that fishing did not have to involve wholesale killing. Fishermen had a choice that hunters did not. As Bud Lilly, one of the West's best-known outfitters and guides, has put it, "It's a lot like golf—you don't have to eat the ball to have a good time."

But for much of its existence, catch-and-release has also had its critics. I first encountered one in Yellowstone about twenty-five years ago when a German visitor indignantly objected to my releasing fish. I did not realize at the time that Europeans were proceeding faster than we were in their protection of what were seen as the rights of animals, and I was shocked that someone could object to a practice that made such good sense in so many ways. At that time I was new to the sport of fly fishing, I didn't think trout tasted all that good anyway, and I was just thrilled that I could fish without interfering much with the food habits of the local eagles, osprey, otters, bears, and other fishers out there. I thought I was on the moral high road, and here came this German chap insisting that I was in the gutter.

There is plenty of easy criticism of the practice of catch-and-release: "So let me get this straight. What you do is, you hook these animals in the mouth and drag them from their environment, right? For all you know they're feeling terrible pain; sometimes you hook them in the tongue, for Heaven's sake. Their frantic struggles, which you seem to find so satisfying and fulfilling, are all the proof any rational person should need that the fish are terrified. Okay, maybe they don't feel pain the way we do. Okay, maybe they can't experience terror with the same level of intellectual and emotional sophistication that we can. But they're doing an excellent imitation of a creature scared entirely out of its mind; why else would they willingly jump again and again from the water into a world where they can't even breathe? So then, after you've put them through that, you don't even *eat* them? It's all just a joke? You just do it for *fun*? You torture these fish and call that sport? How can you *do* that?"

The biggest shock for fishermen the first time we hear this criticism may be that many of these critics find it acceptable to *kill* fish; it's releasing fish that bothers them so much. Killing, they believe, is an understandable use of the fish. Killing the fish is practical and in some ironic sense is even respectful; it keeps the fish in a nice, tidy ethical framework as something we are in charge of and almost have an obligation to consume. Letting the fish go is something much harder to grasp. It suggests that our traditional approach to nature is being violated. We who release fish may couch our behavior in terms of mercy and respect for the fish, but critics suspect some kind of perversion here.

Could be. But sport, like the church or the stock exchange, is an easy institution to lampoon. Sport is most effectively caricatured by trivializing it as something that is only done "for fun." But sport is an ancient human pursuit, like music or cooking or art. Those anonymous artists who painted such powerful portraits of animals in the caves of France twenty thousand years ago probably also engaged in sport. No doubt they had something that could be called fun when they were creating their art, or even when they were hunting (and certainly when they were eating). But to say they simply "had fun" does not do justice to the thing they did, or how it must have felt, or why it mattered to them. The exhilaration of a personal gift that has been painstakingly built into a skill and then exercised with surpassing mastery is far more than fun. Or, perhaps it is just the highest form of fun.

The point here is a matter of culture. For that ancient hunter, there was no absolute separation between painting the animal in the cave, then participating in the hunt of that animal, and then participating in the killing and eating of that animal. These things were all parts of one act. Perhaps none of us today can achieve that wholeness—that integration of so many mysteries—but through study and my own art and my own contacts with the animal, I am willing to piece together whatever of it I can.

Others no longer are. In an essay called "Catch and Deny" in his provocative book *Heart of Home* (1997), Ted Kerasote interviewed a variety of intelligent sportsmen on the matter of catch and release, some of whom have finally quit fishing entirely, either because the scientific evidence that fish do feel pain was piling uncomfortably on their shoulders, or because of some vague fellow-feeling with the fish, or just because it seemed like time. Ted, who has said that "the wading, the casting, the stalking, the picking, the plowing, are the ceremonial means to procure nature's Eucharist," concluded with the uneasiness shared by most of his interviewees and by me.

We fishermen know we're on the defensive here. We do everything we can to reduce the potential for permanently harming the fish. We debarb our hooks to ease the release of the fish. We approach a limited sort of mysticism when we experiment with flies whose hooks are bent closed, or that have no bend at all; unable to hook the fish, we want to see if just the strike alone is enough of a contact (sometimes, almost. . .). We spend more and more time watching and less and less time casting. We suspect, somewhat darkly, that we know where this is headed: to a day when society reverts for a time back to catch-only-if-you-mean-to-kill—a time that will ironically echo the earlier excesses of anglers who killed all too much—and then on to a time when sport fishing goes the way of hunting as an archaic thing people are embarrassed to admit their grandparents did. But we persist because we know, we know damned well, that we are onto something important and that in some troublesome, aching way this catching of fish matters beyond all doubt and all reason.

Of course, "How can you do that?" is not really a question. In order to be a question, a sentence must give some evidence that the speaker is interested in the answer. I am not sure I've ever had a genuine conversation with someone who was outraged about catch-and-release or about the hard realities and violence involved in sport fishing generally. Ideas are not to be exchanged under such circumstances, only rhetorical blows. The question, "How can you do that?" is really a statement: "*I* could not do that, therefore *you* are a brutish fool."

The question is a simplistic challenge about complex and probably unexplainable views of the world. It is what in any other context we would call a personal question. I could ask my questioners about a hundred things that are dear to them ("You drive a car? You pick living wildflowers? You're a Cubs fan? How can you *do* that?"), and they would object that these questions are too big for a quick answer; that their behavior in these activities is the product of their culture and when they do these things they are responding to emotional impulses that I am cheapening by such a superficial question. And yet they seem to find my inability to instantly and completely answer their question about catch-and-release to be proof of my wrongness and—more important to them, I think—of their superior sensitivity and moral fiber.

But there is more to the failure of their question. When they ask, "How can you do that?" and I try to imagine the last thirty years of my life without all those hundreds of glowing days along wild mountain streams all over North America—all the beauty I've absorbed, all the shared and remembered wonder, all the gratitude I've felt not just to the fish but to the rivers they glorify with their presence—I can only turn the question back to them. In my view of the world, and my view of the fish, I am tempted to answer their question by asking them, "Oh, but how can you *not* do that?"

But that's not fair either; it's nearly as bigoted as their original question. If I had to try to answer their question in a meaningful way (rather than in the same quarrelsome and pointless mood that they asked it), I would take a deep breath and say things like this:

> These are matters of the spirit. You may call it a cop-out or a dodge if you like, but these are mysteries in the highest sense of the word. Because they are so insubstantial at the same time that they are so important, I rarely ease off in my testing and questioning of them. I pay attention really hard. I ask myself the same question and I expect an answer. Having told you that, I will tell you that I don't suppose I ever entirely release a fish. I may not eat it, but that does not mean I take nothing from it before I let it go. What I take may be impossible to describe to you, because each time it is different (every catch is a richer experience for all the catches that have gone before), and because you apparently aren't prepared to deal with the possibility that nature affects each of us uniquely and therefore might accommodate different ways of connecting with it. What happens is between me and the fish, between me and what my conscience requires of me. I am not responsible to your conscience. Ultimately, I suspect that "how I can do that" is none of your business, and it is only because I have better manners than you do that I am willing to stand here and let you heap your unreasoning abuse on me.

There are many parts to that moment of taking effect. Some are as simple as the guileless, unaffected behavior of the fish itself, and some are as complicated as knowing that my joy is another creature's terror and another *person's* anguish. We are each different in how we respond to that moment, in how often we need it, and how we feel about the fish that makes it all possible by submitting so involuntarily to our violence.

Early one morning late last fall, before the snow came to stay, I was fishing a local river that hosts a spawning run of brown trout. These fish come up out of bigger water, energized and single-minded in their pursuit of procreation. Here they will meet the occasional osprey or eagle, perhaps an otter once in a while, and me, flailing away with my fly rod in search of the mysterious connection that requires such constant renewal.

The sun was not up. The river glowed in an undulating silver reflection of the pre-dawn light—what Thoreau called "sky water." Between luminous sky and the mirroring river the landscape was a dull, undifferentiated silhouette. Once I cast, I was almost a spectator as the heavy fly plopped up against the opposite bank of the run and made its long swinging inquiries down the current.

It was fairly quiet until the end of the run, where the water broadened and shoaled before draining into a fishless gravel riffle. Just where depth and hope fade, a fish took the fly in mid-swing. It was not a big fish, about fourteen inches long, but it was exceptionally strong for its size. It jumped, then raced from one side of the stream to the other. Then, closer, it jumped again and as small as it was it somehow came down flatly onto the river with the ponderous smack of a much greater bulk. By their very existence, fish can transport us long, wandering miles from where we stand. This fish landed on the river and just for an instant I was in Alaska feeling the rod buck and strain to the pull of a prodigal salmon, and absorbing the warm shock of taking effect at such splendid distances.

But then the trout jerked me back to my own neighborhood. This was still a life and death struggle for it, no matter how far I had drifted in wonder and memory. When it was tired enough I lifted it into clear view in the dull light and saw that shimmering beauty that wherever I find it seems like the most perfect thing I have ever seen and that I so often turn from with a slight twinge of dread that I will never find it again.

It never entered my mind that I could somehow improve on the moment, or better honor nature and the life of this perfect river, by killing the fish and watching all that beauty fade. And the idea of my not being there at all—of trying to enjoy this river and its fish abstractly and remotely or as a bystander on the bank—was well beyond my reach. I cannot fully explain how I can do this, but I know I must.

STUDY TO BE QUIET

Epilogue

STAKES

IF YOU fish long enough, eventually you're going to get it right. You will unpreventably and perhaps to your eventual regret discover the joys of success. The first time, even the first few times, it happens you will probably write it off as proof of the aphorism that even a blind pig finds an acorn now and then.

But if you keep fishing for a long time after that, you're finally going to get it so right that you look like an expert. This has happened to me on a handful of highly visible occasions, and I have explored its awkward consequences in my book *Royal Coachman*. But I left a lot out of that story. The more I think back on my supposed trajectory of refinement as an angler, the more I puzzle over the course I have taken.

The first time I remember getting it right, visibly and for an important audience, was during my first years in Yellowstone. I had been fly fishing for three or four years, and I had a local stream where I could almost always catch something—not because I was such a hot fisherman but because this stream was generous beyond all human dreams of natural benevolence.

As it happened, I had invited some co-workers over for a trout dinner. During the day of the dinner, one of my invitees—an extraordinarily smart and beautiful one, by chance—asked me what kind of trout they were, and I was forced to admit that I didn't know because I had not yet reduced dinner to possession but intended to do so in the hour or so between when I left work and when I'd told my friends to show up. I was a little embarrassed to admit that I wasn't yet ready to serve dinner, but her response was both gratifying and daunting—a wide-eyed expression that said, through its stunning grace and withering sharpness, that I was either an amazingly skilled outdoorsman or an arrogant ass, and that dinner would no doubt show her which.

This really was a good trout stream. Up until the moment when I mentioned that I had not yet bothered to catch the trout, it seemed like a minor detail, like stopping at the store for some milk. But once I experienced the expression on that magical face, the stakes changed. I have never before or since felt so much pressure to hook something, anything, as I did that afternoon.

In the hour or so that I had allowed myself, I did manage to pick up the absolute minimum number of trout needed to fill out the menu. But the pressure to do so was oppressive and the desperate iffiness of the whole enterprise took all sense of accomplishment from doing it. Yes, there were the trout, right there in the pan. But they looked pretty small when I served them. I always wondered if she noticed that as much as I did.

A good twenty-five years later, Marsha and I and two other couples were hiking out from one of Yellowstone's many beautiful small backcountry lakes where we had enjoyed some interesting fishing for small grayling. We were following the little outlet stream, which occasionally dropped over some rocks into a nice pool. One friend, also named Paul, kept his rod assembled for the hike out, and while we watched and offered mildly critical comments, he made some competent casts up toward some deeper water, just a few feet across, right below one of these rocky little waterfalls. He was using a small bead-head nymph, and I could tell that he wasn't quite reaching the good spot. After he'd made a good many casts that fell short of that small stretch of deeper water that spelled fish, I couldn't stand it any longer and asked if he'd mind if I took a try at it. He had all but given up anyway, and cheerfully handed me the rod.

A big problem for him was that the trees were tight behind him, which limited how much room he had for the backcast that would give him the extra few feet of distance needed to reach the right spot. But I also think that he hadn't quite realized that he wasn't reaching the spot anyway. As the little group looked on, I turned and faced away from the little waterfall, threaded a forward cast between the trees, then turned my head and aimed my now suitably long back-cast toward the pool. It took a couple casts to get the range, and I caught a small rainbow. The group was impressed. Then, a cast or two later, I landed the beadhead right under the falling water and it was instantly grabbed by a rainbow of nearly a foot—the fish I knew had to be there and the biggest fish any of us caught all day. When the fish flashed up and splashed in its tiny pool, everyone let out loudly appreciative noises. Paul kept saying, "That was so cool!" and someone else said, "And it wasn't even *his own rod!*"

I must admit, it was worth some mild congratulations, and I also must admit that I felt pretty good about it. The stakes certainly weren't as high as they'd been that day many years before, when I had to produce dinner, but they were high enough to make me smile all the way home.

I fish mostly alone any more and make vast numbers of errors that more than make up for these times when I got it right. But the stakes are different when you fish in the presence of others, or even just in the presence of others' expectations. I find that usually it's my own expectations I most often must wrangle with, and that wrangling has led me into many deliberations about how this whole fishing business is supposed to work. I will conclude this book with one of those deliberations.

There are times when the beauty of a trout stream and the wonder of catching a fish from it are so overpowering that we fall back on the almost desperately metaphorical to explain it. A day on the Madison River comes to mind, when fish were rising to the small mayfly known as the Pale Morning Dun. I don't know that the PMD is my favorite insect—I'm not sure that I could have a favorite animal any more than I could have a favorite song—but the PMD does seem to be the one I try hardest to meet each summer when it emerges in my neighborhood.

This day was, for me at least, a typical PMD experience, which means I had already surrendered to the hard and unfashionable reality that in order to catch any given trout that was feeding on the PMDs I had to try several if not all of the different imitations in my PMD box. The very existence in my vest of a box devoted entirely to variant imitations of this one insect was some indication of my plight. Just because one fish might succumb to a certain of Craig Matthews's excellent sparkle-shucked-compara-poly-whatsits was no indication that the next fish would like that same pattern. It's never like this in the experts' fishing books, but it's always like this for me.

Such persistent exposure to failure and mystery while surrounded by sublime beauty can drive the susceptible angler into highly conjectural realms. After a few decades of reading the self-assured pronouncements of experts for whom days like this don't happen, one admits that one will never inhabit their universe and grasps any straw of comfort floating within reach.

I suspect that many of us have days when we think that the whole hatch-matching business has about it a slight aroma of scam, but I'm not talking here about abandoning the very admirable merit system upon which successful angling is based. Whether one's Parathorax Hyperdun is properly tied, properly cast, properly drifted over the properly sighted trout from the proper angle matters to us in part because it enforces upon us a discipline that earns the reward of a hooked fish. I'm all in favor of earning the reward; that's what the stakes are all about. The poet and essayist Odell Shepard wisely wrote that "angling is in many ways one of the most uncertain of sports, yet the angler may always be perfectly sure of his reward." True enough, but I have yet to experience a day when catching a fish wouldn't help, too.

I suspect that the frustrations and defeats may heighten the effect of those times I've referred to—when all this unspeakably powerful beauty we find in a trout stream suddenly feels like an invitation to fish on some higher plane. The cast goes out there and moves through the beauty of the setting so, well, beautifully, that a higher reward seems in order. Right then we have raised the stakes as high as they will go.

Let's run with that thought for a moment. After a long stretch of disheartening fishlessness it is especially nice to imagine that trout aren't just waiting there, but are brought into being by a certain cast from an angler who, whatever his or her shortcomings, is at that moment so deserving, sincere, and humbled that the river bestows the trout upon him for finer reasons than mere expertise. Perhaps until then trout exists only as an undifferentiated slip of current, and when the angler crosses this mystical threshhold of worthiness, there is the underwater equivalent of "Poof!" as the slip gathers the fluid brilliance of the stream into something firm and lithe that flashes into life and rolls eagerly up to the fly. If you've fished enough clear, wild trout streams, you've certainly had moments when it seemed that the fish materialized out of nothing. Wouldn't it be exciting if that was really what happened, even once in a while—even just once in an angler's life?

It is a testament to the variety of intellect, motivation, and personality among fly fishers that some of them will read the foregoing with condescending pity for any poor soul who succumbs to such a desperate fantasy. But other readers might say, yes, I think that's happened to me, too—or at least I remember a day when I wanted to believe that it could.

This day, I was standing in the stretch of the Madison known locally as the Grasshopper Bank, a place where I have never yet caught a fish on a grasshopper but have often had some success with PMDs. The little mayflies were showing somewhat thinly and I was casting across contrary intervening currents and weed beds to where I thought I saw a fish rise.

There were no other fishermen in the water, but along the shore there was a man in a big pickup truck watching me fish. In my experience, an audience further guarantees failure, but I tried not to blame him.

The trick in this spot was a long drift. If there really was a fish holding in the narrow lane I was trying to cover with my fly, it was a fish that was getting a slow sharp look at each real fly that came over. After five minutes of thrashing preliminaries, I managed a good cast and the fly lit at the head of the several-yard-long-by-ten-inch-wide strip of smooth water between two weed channels and began its drift. It drifted, drifted some more, and then some more. The currents and weeds between me and the fly had a fine time eating up the slack line I'd thrown them, so I began to reach awkwardly to my left, extending the rod farther and farther downstream to give the fly just a few more inches of freedom, then a few more.

When the fly was several feet past my expectations and well below where I'd spotted the rise—and just as I was about to topple over into the water—a trout materialized and grabbed it. The man in the pickup truck let out an appreciative whoop and I dragged the fish in across the weeds and curls of current. All that was left was choosing among my cheery options for explaining to myself why I caught the fish.

This isn't a choice I'd bet money on, but it's not beyond the realm of possibility that this was merely a case of competence. Maybe I actually made such a good cast with such a good fly that I earned the fish the old-fashioned way.

Or maybe it was my persistence. My heroic near-drenching— as I reached and reached and reached some more, and then even more, to keep the fly drifting honestly way beyond normal expectations—might have brought the fly, even if was the wrong fly, into view of some fish I hadn't even suspected was there, who took it just because nobody had reached that spot with any fly whatsoever all year. If that's what happened, I'd still get some credit for doing something right, even though it wasn't the right thing I thought I was doing.

Or maybe the credit really goes to that guy watching me from his truck—the inspiration of a good audience silently cheering me on. After all, I could hardly let myself look like a complete duffer while some absolute stranger who would never see me again was watching, right?

Or, to return to my little fantasy, maybe the river just decided that I'd finally earned a trout, so there one was. Poof!

As an avid reader and defender of science, I know what I should believe about this question, but when it comes to catching a trout I will always have my doubts. Empiricism will only take me so far. So on this occasion, as on countless others along countless streams, I always have and always will leave myself a little space to entertain the mystery. It's good for fishermen not to know absolutely everything that's going on when we make a cast. As Shepard said, it's all about uncertainty.

ACKNOWLEDGMENTS

THANKS FIRST and foremost to Marsha Karle, my spouse and best friend, for encouraging me in this and many other projects, and for putting up with my blank looks when I haven't quite left the work behind at the end of the day. And, more specifically, thanks to Marsha for bringing to life so many moments in these stories and essays with her illustrations. This is our sixth book collaboration as author and artist, and it's always great fun to work together.

Many if not most of the chapters in this book have been reworked considerably during their careers in and out of print. In most cases, this means they have been expanded and updated. A few I've published here in essentially the form they originally appeared. It all depended upon how current they seemed and how they fit in this collection. Some have experienced title changes as well.

Without adding another whole chapter, I couldn't begin to thank all the people I have fished with and all the editors and publishers with whom I have worked, whose friendship, advice, wisdom, and humor have made fly fishing such a special part of my life. I owe them more than I can say, and the very existence of this book is my best hope for expressing my gratitude.

But here are the acknowledgments and thanks I owe for the material in this book. As near as I can tell, "On Monsters" is adapted and enlarged from an essay that first appeared in my book *Pregnant Bears and Crawdad Eyes* (The Mountaineers, 1991).

"My Great Fishing Adventure" previously appeared in *Waterlog*, June/July, 2003.

"Home River" first appeared in my book *Mountain Time* in 1984, and subsequently in both magazine and anthology reprint. It appears here through the courtesy of that book's current (and fourth) publisher, the University of New Mexico Press.

"Jumping Water" first appeared in my book *Mountain Time*, and subsequently in magazine reprint. It appears here through the courtesy of the University of New Mexico Press.

"Rivers in Exile" appeared in the fine anthology, *City Fishing* (Stackpole Books, 2001), edited by Judith Schnell.

"Antlers Aweigh" is adapted from a column I wrote for *Country Journal*, December, 1986, that was later included in my book *Pregnant Bears and Crawdad Eyes* (The Mountaineers, 1991).

"Cairns Pool Reflections" is adapted from the opening paragraphs of a chapter written for *The Elements of Fly Fishing* (Simon & Schuster, 1999), edited by F-Stop Fitzgerald.

"A Lot of Strange Stuff" is not previously published.

"So Long, Sucker" is adapted from an article I wrote for *Backpacker*, December, 1989, that was later included in my book *Pregnant Bears and Crawdad Eyes* (The Mountaineers, 1991).

"The Adams Hatch" is adapted from a column I wrote for *American Angler*, March, 2007. Special thanks for help with this column goes to Michigan writer Jerry Dennis, fishing pals Bud Lilly and Steve Schullery, and Daniel Truckey, executive director of the Grand Traverse Heritage Center, Traverse City, Michigan.

"Crawdad Country" is adapted from a column I wrote for *Country Journal*, October, 1988, that was later included in my book *Pregnant Bears and Crawdad Eyes* (The Mountaineers, 1991).

"The Collateral Catch" is adapted from a column I wrote for *American Angler*, March-April, 2009.

"Drifters" is adapted from a column I wrote for *Country Journal*, August, 1987, that was later included in my book *Pregnant Bears and Crawdad Eyes* (The Mountaineers, 1991).

"Reprehensible Eyes" is a much expanded version of a column I wrote for *American Angler*, November-December, 2008.

"The Fishing of Caribou Creek" appeared in *Fly Fisherman* magazine, July, 2001.

"Brooks River Rainbows" first appeared in my book *Real Alaska: Finding Our Way in the Wild Country* (Stackpole Books, 2001), and is used here through the courtesy of Stackpole Books.

"Farewell Grayling" first appeared in *City Fishing* (Stackpole Books, 2001), edited by Judith Schnell, and later in magazine reprint.

"Dithering Over Dogs" appeared in *Astream* (Skyhorse, 2012), edited by Robert DeMott.

"Should Anglers Re-Invent Themselves?" appeared in *Fly Fisherman*, September, 2005.

"Apologies to the Salmon" appeared in *Backpacker*, January, 1989, and later in my book *Pregnant Bears and Crawdad Eyes* (The Mountaineers, 1991).

"Crazy Coots and Mere Farragos" appeared in *Waterlog*, December 2003/January 2004, and in greatly enlarged form in *The American Fly Fisher*, Fall, 2004.

"How Can You Do That?" is adapted from material that first appeared in my book *Real Alaska: Finding Our Way in the Wild Country* (Stackpole, 2001). The adapted form appeared in *Fly Fisherman*, September, 2003. It appears here through the courtesy of Stackpole Books.

"Epilogue: Stakes" is an expanded version of an article that first appeared in *Big Sky Journal*, Spring, 2009.

NOTES